New Library of Pastoral Care
GENERAL EDITOR: DEREK BLOWS

Brief Encounters

Titles in this series include:

Still Small Voice: An Introduction to Counselling
MICHAEL JACOBS

Letting Go: Caring for the Dying and Bereaved
PETER SPECK AND IAN AINSWORTH-SMITH

Living Alone: The Inward Journey to Fellowship
MARTIN ISRAEL

*Invisible Barriers: Pastoral Care with Physically
Disabled People*
JESSIE VAN DONGEN-GARRAD

*Learning to Care: Christian Reflection on
Pastoral Practice*
MICHAEL H. TAYLOR

Liberating God: Private Care and Public Struggle
PETER SELBY

*Make or Break:
An Introduction to Marriage Counselling*
JACK DOMINIAN

*Meaning in Madness:
The Pastor and the Mentally Ill*
JOHN FOSKETT

*Paid to Care?:
The Limits of Professionalism in Pastoral Care*
ALASTAIR V. CAMPBELL

*Swift to Hear:
Facilitating Skills in Listening and Responding*
MICHAEL JACOBS

*Brief Encounters:
Pastoral Ministry through the Occasional Offices*
WESLEY CARR

New Library of Pastoral Care
GENERAL EDITOR: DEREK BLOWS

BRIEF ENCOUNTERS

*Pastoral Ministry through the
Occasional Offices*

Wesley Carr

(SPCK)

First published in Great Britain 1985
SPCK
Holy Trinity Church
Marylebone Road
London NW1 4DU

British Library Cataloguing in Publication Data

Carr, Wesley
  Brief encounters: pastoral ministry through
  the Occasional Offices. — (New library of
  pastoral care)
  1. Church of England — Clergy   2. Pastoral
  theology
  I. Title   II. Society for Promoting Christian
  Knowledge   III. Series
  253   BV4011

  ISBN 0-281-04179-2

Filmset by Pioneer
Printed in Great Britain by
the Anchor Press, Tiptree

To
The Parochial Clergy and Ministers of the
Diocese of Chelmsford, with whom I have
been privileged to work and minister
1974—1984

Contents

Foreword   ix

Preface   xi

1 Introduction: The Occasional Offices   1

Part One   7
THE THEOLOGICAL AND PASTORAL SIGNIFICANCE
OF THE OCCASIONAL OFFICES

2 Brief Encounters   9
3 Rites and the Church's Task   19
       Church and People   20
       Transitions   22
       Process and Systems   28
4 The Priority of Grace   33
       The World is God's   41
       Christian Life is a Dialectic Existence   42
       Grace is not Cheap   43
       The Priority of Grace   43
5 Christian Sacraments and the Human Life-Cycle   46

Part Two   59
MINISTERING THROUGH THE OCCASIONAL OFFICES

6 Infant Baptism   63
       The Approach   68
       Exploring the Meaning   73
       The Rite   77
       Feed-Back   83

7 Weddings   86
      The Approach   90
      Exploring the Meaning   93
      The Rite   97
      Feed-Back   99
8 Funerals   104
      The Approach   108
      Exploring the Meaning   111
      The Rite   115
      Feed-Back   121

Part Three   125
HANDLING THE PRESSURES FROM THE OCCASIONAL OFFICES

9 The Minister: Pressure and Resources   127
      Pressure from Time   127
      Pressure from the Church   128
      Pressure from the Minister   130
      Pressure from Emotions   131
      Pressure from Theology   132
      Theological Indications for Ministry through
         the Occasional Offices   134

Index   141

Foreword

The *New Library of Pastoral Care* has been planned to meet the needs of those people concerned with pastoral care, whether clergy or lay, who seek to improve their knowledge and skills in this field. Equally, it is hoped that it may prove useful to those secular helpers who may wish to understand the role of the pastor.

Pastoral care in every age has drawn from contemporary secular knowledge to inform its understanding of man and his various needs and of the ways in which these needs might be met. Today it is perhaps the secular helping professions of social work, counselling and psychotherapy, and community development which have particular contributions to make to the pastor in his work. Such knowledge does not stand still, and a pastor would have a struggle to keep up with the endless tide of new developments which pour out from these and other disciplines, and to sort out which ideas and practices might be relevant to his particular pastoral needs. Among present-day ideas, for instance, of particular value might be an understanding of the social context of the pastoral task, the dynamics of the helping relationship, the attitudes and skills as well as factual knowledge which might make for effective pastoral intervention, and perhaps most significant of all, the study of particular cases, whether through verbatim reports of interviews or general case presentation. The discovery of ways of learning from what one is doing is becoming increasingly important.

There is always a danger that a pastor who drinks deeply at the well of a secular discipline may lose his grasp of his own pastoral identity and become 'just another' social worker or counsellor. It in no way detracts from the value of these professions to assert that the role and task of the pastor are quite unique among the helping professions and deserve to be

ix

clarified and strengthened rather than weakened. The theological commitment of the pastor and the appropriate use of his role will be a recurrent theme of the series. At the same time the pastor cannot afford to work in a vacuum. He needs to be able to communicate and co-operate with those helpers in other disciplines whose work may overlap, without loss of his own unique role. This in turn will mean being able to communicate with them through some understanding of their concepts and language.

Finally, there is a rich variety of styles and approaches in pastoral work within the various religious traditions. No attempt will be made to secure a uniform approach. The Library will contain the variety, and even perhaps occasional eccentricity, which such a title suggests. Some books will be more specifically theological and others more concerned with particular areas of need or practice. It is hoped that all of them will have a usefulness that will reach right across the boundaries of religious denomination.

DEREK BLOWS
Series Editor

Preface

This book has been written out of experience of public ministry and critical reflection and study of it with clergy and ministers in a variety of contexts. Apart from a period of two years, most of my ministry has been rooted in a parochial context, but with sufficient distance from it to be able to examine it. While Sir Henry Stephenson Fellow in the Department of Biblical Studies at Sheffield University I assisted the late Geoffrey Needham in the parish of Ranmoor. Chelmsford Cathedral, my present base, is a parish church cathedral. The study of pastoral experience has been a major concern for the past ten years, originally as Deputy Director of the Chelmsford Cathedral Centre for Research and Training, but, since its closure, with a small group of interested people. They have all contributed, knowingly and unknowingly.

The aim of this series is to be of interest to people other than clergy and ministers. In the nature of the case, however, the performance of the occasional offices and the questions they raise are very ecclesiastical. I have, therefore, tried to emphasize the place of these rites in the spectrum of pastoral care, as this is offered by a wide range of individuals and institutions. Special attention has been given to providing additional material through the references in the footnotes. This has two aims: firstly, to encourage people other than the church's ministers to see where their specialisms might link to the church's work through the occasional offices; and secondly, to try and enlarge the horizons of the clergy's operations, which often seem mundane.

The word 'ministry' is high on the church's agenda. It is a notoriously problematic term, which both generates and disguises confusions. I have not tried to provide detailed definitions for it, but hope that clarity about ministry may emerge through reflecting on the church's work and its modern environment. The work stands or falls in its own right. But the approach may be unfamiliar to some, and I hope, therefore, I may be forgiven the presumption of mentioning an earlier book— *The Priestlike Task* (London, SPCK, 1985). Further material on the task of the church and the role of the clergy may be found there, together with some of the theoretical ideas which undergird the present argument.

Other terminology is also a difficulty in contemporary writing about ministry. For the sake of variety 'minister', 'vicar', 'clergyman' and 'pastor' have been used interchangeably. The question of gender is not easily resolved. Here masculine pronouns refer to all ministers, male and female, unless the context makes it clear that at present this is unfortunately not possible.

Inevitably this writing betrays a perspective drawn chiefly from the Church of England, but I trust that it is not blinkered. Colleagues from other churches have been consulted. And the attentive reader might discern that my own Christian origins are not Anglican.

The ideas and attitudes discussed in this book derive from many sources, most of them necessarily unacknowledged. Harold Frankham, Vicar of Luton and later Provost of Southwark, taught me the importance of this fundamental ministry for the wider aims of a parish church. The clergy of the Diocese of Chelmsford, to whom this book is dedicated as a mark of genuine affection and admiration, have given me much. Two of them in particular— Michael Fox (Vicar of All Saints, Chelmsford) and Timothy Stevens (Rector of Canvey Island)— have usefully commented on an early draft. I also owe special thanks to Peter Marshall, Canon Residentiary of Chelmsford Cathedral, for his many contributions as associate, colleague and consultant. My wife, Natalie, knew exactly when to stay out of my way and when to be on hand for the drudgery of proof reading. All of these have stimulated reflection, provided evidence, and offered ideas about this ministry. The inadequacies and inaccuracies, however, remain my responsibility.

One person on reading a draft commented that it made the job of the minister seem very demanding, very responsible, and very important. It is. And if this small work enables my fellow clergy to a better understanding of their role and greater clarity about their theology and ministry, I shall be honoured.

Wesley Carr
December 1984
Chelmsford Cathedral

ABBREVIATIONS

References are given in full. When titles are cited a second time or more, an abbreviated title is used. Two abbreviations, however, are employed throughout:

ET English Translation.
Books are cited only in English, and details of the original are not given.

TPT Wesley Carr, *The Priestlike Task* (London, SPCK, 1985).

ONE

Introduction: The Occasional Offices

The rites which are used as occasion demands—the occasional offices—are to many people more familiar than those which comprise the regular worship of the church. In the Book of Common Prayer eight such offices are provided: Baptism, Confirmation, Matrimony, the Visitation of the Sick, the Communion of the Sick, Burial, the Churching of Women, and the Commination. Today, however, for practical purposes the issues of ministry through these occasional offices arise in connection with the baptism of infants, weddings and funerals. When we begin to think about these, ritual, religion and rites become entangled. Theology, psychology, sociology and anthropology vie for attention, so that we feel overwhelmed by

> Greek endings, each the little passing-bell
> That signifies some faith's about to die.[1]

For all this, the local church and minister experience demands being made which, however they are interpreted and from whatever perspective they are explained, still have to be dealt with. Explanation is not necessarily the means to salvation; neither is confusion. We may, therefore, on the one hand acknowledge the sense of confusion that may be generated in us when our attention is directed to the theory and practice of pastoring. But on the other hand we may also recognize that merely to continue to act without trying to understand is irresponsible. We need to find a means of living in and contributing to the richly problematic area of human life which the church encounters through these occasional offices, without surrendering to the reductionism implicit in some social scientific interpretation or theological approaches. 'Septic human relationships cannot survive in an

1

antiseptic bath of psycho-social formaldehyde.'[2] Ministers, therefore, need to seek a model of pastoral ministry by which to chart their way through the seas of interpretation now available to them and through the waves of demands which strike the local minister in his parish or church.

This book is one of a series on pastoral care and practice. It is not intended as a contribution to the wealth of technical literature on rites, rituals or social customs. Nor is it particularly concerned with the theology of the sacraments. But neither topic can be omitted. Indeed, one of the continuing themes of this essay is the way in which content and context may be too quickly separated in order to escape problems which have to be faced for effective ministry. If a problem is avoided, the chances are that an opportunity will also be missed. Context and content interact. For example, at different moments in their lives a couple may say to each other, 'I love you'. The words are identical, whether they are those of nervous first love, the ardently newly-wed, the unsettling period of mid-life crisis, or of contented old age. But the content of the words changes according to which of these contexts applies. But the context, too, is altered by the fact of the words being uttered. They themselves contribute to the relationship and thus make their own utterance more or less possible. In the present study we shall address this interaction of theology and practice, or of word and context. This may mean that at times major issues may appear to be left aside. But in the course of the total argument I hope to cover the key issues which arise in connection with the occasional offices, although with the clear recognition that on a subject so sensitive as this, major differences are bound to remain.

The occasional offices are a major facet of the church's pastoral ministry. This word 'pastoral' is widely used in contemporary discussion and writing on ministry. It seems so frequently attached to some other word—ministry, care, theology, practice—that it assumes an Alice in Wonderland aspect of apparently meaning everything but usually meaning nothing. When in 1978 the cardinals met in Rome after the sudden death of Pope John Paul I, pastoral factors loomed large. Having chosen one pope for his pastoral gifts, they

seemed to think that they should find another. Peter
Hebblethwaite graphically describes how the discussions
developed. 'Pastoral' began to be applied to every aspect of
ministry. At first it meant 'coming from a diocese', but
gradually those in tribunals, lawyers, members of the Curia,
and ultimately all the cardinals were described as 'pastoral'.
'Thus "pastoral" became a broken-backed word.'[3] Another,
less exalted, example of how this term may be used as a
catch-all is taken from the programme for a county youth
camp:

> I would like to thank the camp leader, his village helpers
> and leaders who have supervised a varied programme of
> activities and dealt with the pastoral side of the camp.

Many similar examples could be cited to illustrate how
'pastoral' tends to be used to cover every eventuality which is
not dealt with under some other heading. One area which is
germane to the present discussion is that of pastoral
counselling. This phrase seems to allow the notion of
counselling to be invested with theological aura and thus
incorporated uncritically into the range of Christian ministry.
As a result ministers in their enthusiasm seem to become
preoccupied with crises and casualties, to whom they feel
that they can offer a professionally competent pastoral
counselling ministry. But one response which is sometimes
heard from ministers who have acquired such training is that
they seem not to meet people. Having acquired the skills of
counselling, they discover that people do not come for counsel.
Thus for them is confirmed one of the prevailing fantasies of
ministers. Just as doctors think they are underpaid, so clergy
believe often that they are unwanted. The continuing demand
for the occasional offices, which will be explored in detail
later, suggests that people may desire the church's ministry
(though not necessarily counselling) while the church's
ministers find it increasingly difficult to perceive that such
encounters are ministry. It may be that counselling skills are
being sought to authenticate a pastoral ministry, such as has
traditionally been offered, as a substitute for the loss of a
theological justification for it. If counselling has been assigned
a theological aura, so too, perhaps, theology has similarly

been invested with a counselling halo. The apparent ignorance of both gospel and church on the part of those who approach the minister may confirm in the minister some sense of a lost theological framework. Confronted, therefore, with counselling assumptions in himself and theological ignorance in the applicants, the minister may find the contemporary requirements of the occasional offices almost too complicated to bear.[4]

There is additionally a question about the role of the minister which is raised by these encounters. The minister's own understanding of his role may seem far from the belief that people display about it. And the meaning of the gospel for them seems to be different from what he hopes it is. Personal problems compound the stress. Dealing with profound human emotions in a raw state, the minister finds his own self also disturbed. Facing a couple with the meaning of marriage brings his own marriage to mind. Committing a corpse to the ground or to the flames reminds him of his own mortality. And all this in a context where simple theological issues suddenly become profound and questioning: Is this what God intends mankind to be? Did Christ really die for this world? Is the Kingdom of God any different from the Church? The occasional offices constitute a draining demand on time, energy and emotion. They raise questions about the theological norms and internally determined customs of the contemporary church. And even in the face of the current secularism in British society, they remain a demand with which, at least for the time being, the Christian church has to deal.

This book is divided into three parts. First there is a general consideration of the occasional offices from a series of perspectives. This includes reflection on the church and its task in society, with some of the consequences of this for its theology and practice. The second part consists of studies of the three primary offices—infant baptism, weddings and funerals. The discussion here is practical. A final chapter draws together some of the pressures on the minister himself and what these may signify, as well as how they may be used in ministry. The divisions are for convenience, but the argument, as I have suggested already, is to be read as a single whole.

Notes

1. Robert Browning, *Bishop Blougram's Apology.*
2. Aidan Kavanagh, 'Life-cycle events, civic ritual and the Christian', in D. Power and L. Maldonado, ed., *Liturgy and Human Passage, Concilium* 112 (1979), pp. 14ff.
3. Peter Hebblethwaite, *The Year of the Three Popes* (London, Collins, 1978), p. 135.
4. David Martin, *A General Theory of Secularisation* (Oxford, Blackwell, 1978), pp. 278ff.

PART ONE

The Theological and Pastoral Significance of the Occasional Offices

TWO

Brief Encounters

In any encounter with someone or some group around a baptism, wedding or funeral, the minister touches something deep about life but necessarily does so in a brief, temporary and transitory engagement. There are few, if any, churches that could encourage such meetings with people at length and in depth. Time is always at a premium for the minister. But, as will be seen, it is unlikely that the applicants would wish for much more, even if it were available. In the nature of the case with the occasional office the encounter is fleeting. In this chapter we shall examine these brief encounters from the perspective of the minister and of those seeking his ministry.

The minister, unless he deliberately isolates himself from any engagement with people in the community at an instinctive level, is bound to be thrust into the midst of people's expectations of what he ought to do. He regards himself as a minister of the gospel, even at times in danger of becoming a professional Christian. But when approached for the ministry of an occasional office, he finds that his Christian gospel seems of little interest. He is immersed in implicit or folk religion. This topic has been widely discussed.[1] People recognize in themselves experiences which they may feel somehow to be 'religious'. From time to time they seek ritual expression for these feelings and for that purpose regard themselves as members of the church.[2] If they feel rejected at this point they become angry, but—and this is an important facet of the occasional offices—will often persist in finding what they want by going to another church, and, if need be, more than one.

Nineteenth-century intellectual confidence in the demise of religion has proved misplaced.[3] Indeed today it sometimes seems that it is now the churches themselves which chiefly believe, and act upon that belief, that religion is finished. Polls are notoriously unreliable, but even if the figures are read at their face value, they show that a large number of people still look to the church for a ministry through the occasional offices.[4] And where such figures are low, there is now the suspicion that the churches by their behaviour may be encouraging them to be so. Of all people ministers should not be fooled into believing in some historical inevitability about the decline of religious expression. They may well at times ask themselves whether their appeals to sociological theories of secularization, the rites of passage, and the like, may not be attempts to explain away or rationalize an uncomfortable part of their ministry.

The heavy demand of the occasional offices—both in the sense of being time-consuming as well as in the way in which it puts pressure upon the minister's Christian motivation and understanding—contrasts pointedly with the apparent unproductiveness of such encounters. Even if in the long term a correlation were discerned between this ministry and church membership, there still seems to be no immediate pay-off. In practice people rarely seem to join the congregation or contribute to funds. There is a discontinuity between the criteria of successful ministry that tend to be used by the church as an institution, with its statistical tables and quotas, and the amount of time and energy devoted to people in this immature state of religious expectation. One defence against this is to rationalize the issue, either in terms of why people do not join or in terms of creating conditions which would make it difficult for them to join, even if they wished. What, then, is the place of such a ministry, with this public 'failure' and the guilt (sometimes anger) that is generated in the minister, as he is caught between his gospel and the ordinary life of people?

On top of these pressures from the church and from within, the minister further encounters the belief that such ministries are engagement with people who are outside the church and that they therefore constitute prime opportunities for mission and evangelism. These two words are currently in vogue, and as such they are traps for the unwary. Every meeting with someone who is not a member of the church, so it is assumed,

is a moment of mission. But to any sensitive minister the
encounter around a baptism, wedding or funeral, scarcely
feels like that. For mission is essentially an aggressive activity.
The missionary is sent to an alien environment in order to
bring to it something new. We might even say that applicants
for the occasional office present themselves as the missionary.
They seem to bring to, what is for them, an alien world of the
church and the vicar a believed reality from everyday life,
about which the vicar is supposed to know little and
understand less. The tables are turned on him as the
applicants set the agenda. Indeed, they come to some extent
because over the centuries the church has bid them come,
sometimes chased after them to come, and generally provided
the normal means for ritual expression of aspects of human
life. 'In the realm of the imagination, once something
extraordinary is produced, it is never lost. Changes in culture
only widen the expressive repertoire of mankind.'[5] In such
meetings the minister feels that he is more likely to be used
than to be able to use the occasion for some form of
evangelism or mission. And when he tries to evangelize, he
sometimes finds himself in an odd position: whatever he
says, people will affirm, but there is no engagement with
what he conceives as his message. Frustration results. To be
able to live with this, a profounder understanding of the
nature of Christian ministry is required.

The key to understanding ministry lies neither within the
church nor within the minister. It comes from seeing that the
church and the minister are available for ministry because of
the way in which they interact with their environment.[6] The
persistence of people in the face of attempts to discourage
them is one of the remarkable aspects of these encounters.
Every hoop will be gone through and many a demand endured
in order to achieve the desired result. Unless this process is
appreciated as having some validity in itself, a downward
spiral in the relationship between the minister and the
applicants ensues. If he is thinking in terms of an opportunity
to proclaim the full content of the Christian gospel, he will
find an increasing sense that his words and interpretations
are neither being heard nor resisted. The resulting sense of
guilt at failing to preach the gospel, compounded with some

feeling of having let God down, may produce anger. This usually issues in one of two fashions. He may become angry with the people, who then feel violently rejected, even if the minister has been polite and, as he might say, pastoral. Or he may become angry with himself or with God, which, when such introversion occurs, leads to apathy.

When the structures of the church and social life change, there is a tendency to replace what we might describe as a 'natural' ministerial function with a professional one. The minister, feeling that he is deprived of his distinctive, and to him familiar, role, may seek personal affirmation by acquiring new skills. These tend to be found in the modern human sciences. Through using these he may discover that his own feelings may not be produced merely by his personal emotional state. He may become aware of other factors in people and of the way in which he functions in the larger networks of human relationships. By appreciating these experiences he may, so the argument runs, become a better minister. There is truth in this, and many courses are currently offered to assist ministers to develop and use such understanding.[7] There is also little doubt that contemporary approaches to pastoral care through counselling theory and skills can and do serve the church's ministry. Yet care is needed, not least when the minister is involved with people through the occasional offices, lest superficial connections are made between counselling ideas and Christian ministry. This is especially easy in view of the way that Christian themes and illustrations are widely employed in psychotherapeutically oriented writing and of the apparent correspondence of ideas between applied theology and counselling. The seminal work, for example, of Truax and Carkhuff directs attention away from techniques towards empathy, openness and non-possessive love. They also speak of the outcome of counselling in terms of growth and healing.[8]

Similar to some ministerial ideals as these notions may be, the counselling presumption may not lightly be made when considering Christian ministry. It represents something deeper in contemporary culture than some may realize. In looking in this direction, the minister may be aligning himself, probably uncritically and almost certainly unwittingly, with the prevailing mores rather than using a culturally neutral stance in the service of his ministry.[9] His attitude conveys to those who approach him messages about the assumptions that he may be making about them. But by their sheer continuance the occasional offices seem to represent a desire for some rite which is precisely not some cultural norm. To come to the minister for the performance of a rite and then find oneself caught up with another 'expert', like the doctor, or the marriage guidance counsellor, or the school adviser, may be a diminishing experience which is contrary to the main thrust of the gospel.[10] The minister may covertly encourage such encounters, because the apparent stability of the therapeutically ordered culture may itself be a romantic longing for control or power.[11] But if this were exposed and labelled 'Christendom' or 'triumphalism', he would shun it.

The confidence of the minister in the Christian gospel has in this argument to be assumed as his primary motivation for ministering. When, however, he meets those who have specific expectations of one particular role, such as that of vicar, he also requires some confidence in that role. That in turn derives from such belief as he may have in the church, not as a theological construct or as an idealized divine institution, but as a human organization. The occasional offices bring him face to face with earthy realities of human beings, the day-to-day church, and above all himself. A further danger of the counselling presumption is that he may use it as a defence against these legitimate pressures upon him and upon his ministry. What may be valuable in awakening human sensitivity in the minister and acuteness in listening to what is being conveyed to him, may become not so much a tool in service of his ministry, but its substance.

At a practical level, too, the counselling presumption may make the minister less effective in ministry through the occasional offices. In therapy the emphasis is upon listening, time and depth. A series of meetings is more usual than one brief encounter. There is also a sense of the need to see through a complete process. And, most importantly, this model assigns prime importance to the one-to-one meeting. But, as will be seen, although instances of ministry through the occasional offices sometimes present themselves as such encounters, they are rarely, if ever, so. They are always social events, and crucial to this ministry is the institutional role of the church and of its ministers. The person requesting some such rite comes to a church or minister which is believed to be handling not only the realities of existence but also the meaning of life itself and its ultimate significance. The minister's role, therefore, is largely assigned to him, and is one which on the whole he does not determine and which cannot be aligned with those of other 'experts'. For the minister, then, the occasional offices represent problematic instances of ministry which may not simply be categorized away by any theological or professional stance which does not itself derive from the specific interaction of church and people in this basic, almost primitive, way. They, therefore, challenge not only his gospel and human sensitivity, but at the same time undermine some of the assumptions about itself that the contemporary church seems prone to make. But for all the difficulty that they present, the occasional offices may be for the minister the touchstone of ministry, standing as they do at key points of interaction between the church and its human environment.[12]

We may now turn briefly to the way in which the applicant regards this brief encounter. Later the particular instances will be examined in more detail; here we merely note some generally observable facets of these engagements. First, it is a request that something be done *for* them. The preposition is significant: it is not something done *with* them or *to* them, but is done on their behalf. This is a key insight, if the church is not to fall into self-aggrandisement in this area. Rites are not given for all time. They change in the light of cultural circumstances, even though the change is slow and hard to perceive. Rites of passage are naturally thought of as social anthropologists have determined them. They are transition rites, usually associated with major moments in human social movement.[13] Given expression through religious ritual they seem almost immutable. But rites of passage do change. For example, it seems that for some marriage has ceased to be regarded as such a rite. It has been replaced by the acquisition of a mortgage and the birth of the first child.[14] The ritualizing of living at home, moving through marriage to setting up a new household is a comparatively recent development in Western Europe. It may be, for example, that contemporary concern for and interest in the family is a response to the aggressive, competitive individualism of industrial capitalism.[15] The church, therefore, or any other body engaged in ritual, does not create the rite. It has rather to be alert to the nature of the request that it perform something for people.

The minister's experience of the occasional office is of a one-off event, which is extracted from people's everyday life and with which they seem to burden the church. From the applicant's point of view, however, the vision is different. The ceremony is merely one event in a continuing process. What for the minister is a brief line in a full diary is, for those concerned, almost a timeless moment. It links in a series of other such moments in the family history, sometimes almost as if there had been no intervening period. It is intriguing, for example, to note how each ceremony is often contrasted and compared with similar occasions which date back through family history. The photograph album (and maybe now the film and video) has replaced the family Bible as a record. But there is still the record. For baptisms an old christening robe may be brought out, and weddings often have the bride wearing something handed down through the family. Vicars are recalled with favour or disfavour. To appreciate this a distinction may be drawn between temporal, or diary, time and experienced time. They are qualitatively different, and the minister who fails to perceive this may find himself operating with the wrong time-scale and feel the associated dislocation.[16]

A second aspect of these brief encounters is the way in which, however humble the occasion, it seems to indicate a sense of something more. A man comes to the cathedral dressed in motor-cycling gear. From his leathers he produces a delicate gold cross, not a cheap one, and asks me to bless it. It is to be given to a girl—not his girl friend—as a memento of her boy-friend, who was killed in a crash. When we talk—inevitably briefly—many issues arise: genuine affection for the dead friend, whom he can now only contact through the man's closest friend, the girl; a concern for the girl, lest she should feel that no one cares; some vague feeling in himself of the need to express the worth of his own life; and against all these (and no doubt many other issues) the pervasive background of the nearness of death, even to a young man in his twenties. Why should the cross be blessed? Somewhere he dredges up the view that this is right and proper and that the cross has something to do with death. But beyond that he can only be inarticulate. But the major step for him was to come into a cathedral, ask for a priest, have one summoned, and then talk to him. Many clergy can give similar examples. Similar requests arise over exorcism and the blessing of houses. The line here narrows between full-blown spiritism, from which most people recoil, and a simple belief that there is something 'there' and that it has to be acknowledged. What the pastor will do in any particular circumstance will vary. What all these have in common, however, is the sense of some ultimate in the midst of life. There is a human need to be able to 'name something'.[17] If this were not possible, then life would degenerate into an undifferentiated continuum. In the face of this prospect, however, the longing for order, feeble though the grasp of it may be, underlies much human behaviour. There is a link between this and the Christian gospel, but to understand this ministers need to acknowledge theologically what is being interpreted through the contemporary human sciences.

Thirdly, from the applicant's point of view the key to any encounter over the occasional offices is the rite itself and the ritual that accompanies it. Ritual consists of formalized acts which express things through their symbolic quality.[18] This is why there sometimes appears to be a disjunction between the expectations of the minister and those of the people. The minister tends to think that the liturgy itself, which he controls, is a sufficient symbol. People, however, invest much in apparently meaningless pieces of ritual: whether the baby cries or not; numerous additions to the burial service — words, ivy leaves, postures; and a very clear example from the marriage service — the use of the stole. At the joining of hands and pronouncement of the marriage there is no rubric for the binding of the hands with the stole. It is, however, often done, and has become 'a popular action in the sense that at this point the congregation leans forward to watch, then relaxes with an audible sigh'.[19] Such additional rituals are not meaningless, but they represent the importance that the people invest in ritual for its own sake. Unless the minister can grasp this, then dissatisfaction and confusion will result for all. Recently a minister in a church in a new town found he could not find a second curate. The church was in the evangelical tradition, and all the candidates felt that their ministry should be to churches full of people whom they could offer a teaching ministry. They could not see any special value in the fifty or so weddings that they would have to perform each year, not to mention other rites, and the resulting contact with families in the area. They were all unhappy with the expectation of rites. This story exposes some of the difficulty in appreciating and thinking about the occasional offices. If the church was to remain and work in that area, at work with the gospel among the parishioners, the ministers needed not merely sociological interpretation into the nature and function of rites, but a means of assigning them theological value as a facet of common human experience. Without that, any suggestions on how to perform these rituals are likely to fall on deaf ears, and rightly so. The formation of the minister and his motivation in the light of the church's work in its environment is the crucial factor. It is, therefore, to a short consideration of such issues that we now turn.

Notes

1. *TPT*, ch. 4. Bruce Reed, *The Dynamics of Religion* (London, DLT, 1978), ch. 5. John Habgood, *Church and Nation in a Secular Age* (London, DLT, 1983), ch. 5. More technical discussion may be found in D. Martin, *A Sociology of English Religion* (London, Heinemann, 1967); R. Towler, *Homo Religiosus* (London, Constable, 1974), especially ch. 8; L. Schneider, ed., *Religion, Culture and Society* (New York, Wiley, 1964).
2. D. Hay, *Exploring Inner Space* (Harmondsworth, Pelican, 1982).
3. Daniel Bell, 'The return of the sacred', *British Journal of Sociology* 28 (1977), pp. 419ff.
4. W. S. F. Pickering, 'The persistence of rites of passage; towards an explanation', *British Journal of Sociology* 25 (1974), pp. 63ff.

5. Bell, 'Return', p. 425.
6. Reed, *Dynamics,* especially ch. 7. *TPT,* chaps. 1—3.
7. Leslie Virgo, 'First aid in pastoral care: skills in pastoral care', *Expository Times* 96 (1984), pp. 4ff.
8. C. B. Truax and R. R. Carkhuff, *Toward an Effective Counselling and Psychotherapy* (Chicago, Aldine, 1967).
9. Maurice North, *The Secular Priests* (London, Allen & Unwin, 1972), pp. 288ff.
10. Peter Selby, *Liberating God* (London, SPCK, 1983), pp. 40ff.
11. See Adolf Guggenbuhl-Craig, *Power and the Helping Professions* (New York, Spring, 1971).
12. *TPT,* ch. 6.
13. A large amount of literature is available. Two seminal works are A. van Gennep, *The Rites of Passage* (ET London, RKP, 1960) and V. Turner, *The Ritual Process* (London, RKP, 1969). See also the essays in M. Gluckmann, ed., *Essays on the Ritual of Social Relations* (Manchester, Manchester University Press, 1962).
14. F. Musgrove and R. Middleton, 'Rites of passage and the meaning of age in three contrasted social groups: professional footballers, teachers and Methodist ministers', *British Journal of Sociology* 32 (1981), pp. 38ff.
15. J. Beattie, 'Ritual and social change', *Man* n.s.l. (1966), pp. 60ff.
16. The way that time is conceived is more significant than those who live by the diary and the clock realize. See E. R. Leach, 'Time and false noses', in *Rethinking Anthropology* (London, Athlone Press, 1963).
17. Kathleen Bliss, *The Future of Religion* (Harmondsworth, Pelican, 1969).
18. J. Beattie, 'On understanding ritual', in B. Wilson, ed., *Rationality* (Oxford, Blackwell, 1970).
19. Diana L. Barker, 'A proper wedding', in M. Corbin, ed., *The Couple* (Harmondsworth, Pelican, 1978), p. 73.

THREE

Rites and the Church's Task

There is a well-known series of pictures which, depending on how they are viewed, convey different images—an old woman or a beautiful demi-mondaine; a snow-covered mountainside or the face of a man; and, probably best known of all, a duck or a rabbit. They are used to distinguish between 'seeing' and 'seeing as'. This distinction is useful for understanding aspects of the church's day-to-day ministry. No human encounter is ever as simple as it first appears. Pastors, therefore, need to be able to perceive as best they may what is being asked and expected from them, if they are not to disappoint people, annoy them, or, at worst, damage them. For some ministers this means training; others seem to do it naturally. But the point of reflection is the same for all. This chapter is about 'seeing as', using this as an approach to investigating what appears familiar. The study is the outer framework of the pastor's ministry. His inner motivation and theological resource we shall examine in the next chapter. The argument is not a series of hints on how to manage pastoral encounters, but rather it offers a way of interpreting evidence, which may enable the minister to respond to the expectations of those who approach him. In other words, a way of analysing pastoral ministry is proposed, particularly as this concerns the occasional offices.

Care, however, is needed with the idea of analysis. For it is possible to decline into a form of reductionism which dehumanizes people in the interests of preserving the integrity of the minister or the believed sanctity of the church. Yet careful analysis can enable the minister to place himself and the people in a context and thus be specific about the task of ministry. One well-known instance is found in work done on the bereavement process. Several researchers have discerned four major stages to this: shock, control, regression and adaptation.[1] The value of this analysis for the minister is that it provides a framework within which to try and set the distracting experiences of the bereaved and thus hold some sense of reality on their behalf. But two obvious dangers also emerge. First, the minister may take the analysis as a basis for technique and as a result may reduce in his own mind any individual bereavement to part of a predetermined process. Second, in the absence of anything else to say or do, the minister might be tempted to expound this framework to the bereaved person as a believed means of reassurance and comfort. Against the first approach stand the arguments of the authors themselves that every bereavement is necessarily unique; and against the second we may set the gospel message that life and death are more than mere conformity to any process. But in spite of such obvious pitfalls such an analysis can profitably inform the minister, not least because at a point of stress it may enable him to recall that human experience is something other than merely the presentation of symptoms.

There are three parts to the argument of this chapter. First, the question is examined as to why people approach the church for such ministry. The occasional offices are chiefly moments when those with fringe or apparently no involvement with the church arrive expecting some service. Even in modern Britain the figures remain significant.[2] Some enquiry into the phenomenon, therefore, is needed. To dismiss it as superstition may not suffice. Second, we shall consider human life in terms of transitions. Third, a model will be offered for analysing the interaction between church and people as a way of giving shape to that which often appears to be unmanageable.

Church and People

Why people approach the church at all has been discussed in a number of recent publications.[3] Whatever the theological interpretation of the church that may at any time be dominant, the persistence of the occasional offices and the demand for them regularly reminds the minister that there is also a continuing social interaction which contributes to the idea of the church in people's minds.

> There is inevitably an element of childlike dependency in the relationship to the church, and thus to its representatives, in that to some extent they are asked to solve the insoluble, cure the incurable, and make reality go away.[4]

This statement does not imply that people feel dependent in a conscious fashion. The notion of dependency is used in a value-free way to describe the dynamic interrelation between people and church or minister. It is not, therefore, a description of individual behaviour. Pervasive dependency — which we might call 'a culture of dependency' — is an aspect of the corporate life of society which the church, along with other institutions, is invited to handle. When, therefore, people come for one of the occasional offices, they are bringing with them more than they know. There is customarily no clear request or understanding of what is wanted: 'It seems right', 'It's the proper thing to do.' These, and similar, responses, which are the bane of the minister, sum up incomprehensible feelings, which the person cannot analyse or fully understand. One reason for this is that at one level they are acting on behalf of more people than they realize — what is loosely called 'society'. People's behaviour towards and around the church carries surprising implications for others.[5]

Such an interpretation could clearly be a form of wish fulfilment on the part of the clergy to reassure themselves that, in spite of the apparent decline in religious observance, they nevertheless still stand for something important. The evidence needs constant testing. But many, and not the clergy alone, are still surprised by the inexplicable feelings which seem to arise around such events as weddings or funerals. Other material comes from parishes in which the church has pursued a very rigorist baptismal policy. Various aspects of ministry in the community appear to have been inhibited because of the anger which becomes diffused throughout the parish, not only among those with babies and children, but more generally. We shall examine this in detail later, but it is worth noting that in such places clergy often use hostile language when referring to their parishioners, while they seek personal gratification and professional legitimation within an eclectic congregation. This observation derives from an Anglican perspective, but so far as I can judge from colleagues in other churches, similar instances can be found elsewhere. But even this behaviour, whether approved of or not, evidences the fundamental point that the church as an institution exists by interaction with its human, emotional environment. This relationship is characterized by dependency, as this has been outlined, and this foundation undergirds the following arguments in this book.

Transitions

Shakespeare's Jaques describes seven ages for men, as they journey from distress to momentary glory and finally to 'mere oblivion', playing their brief parts on the world's stage: infant, schoolboy, lover, soldier, ruler, old man, and corpse.[6] Graduation from one stage to the next is not marked by a special rite of passage. They are taken as self-evident progressions, *mutatis mutandis,* for every human being. But the idea lying behind this description of ordered development runs deep in the psyche. Shakespeare's dramatic outline may usefully be compared with that offered by the psychoanalyst, Erik Erikson.[7] For Shakespeare the progression is through a series of marked points. Erikson indicates that these historical moments are related to a continuing, and sometimes repeated, series of points of growth, as the individual becomes more aware of his identity. For example, the birth of a child is an event which has to be named in the life history of that child, of the parents, of the extended family, and so on. The birth also marks a profound shift in the interpersonal relationship of the parents, which changes from that of a couple to that of a trio. New relationships are created which will affect a whole series of subsequent, and at the time unknowable, relationships. So of Martin Luther, Erikson points out that the relationship of father to son and of mother to son not only affected the individuality of the boy but also future relationships between himself and others, indeed between himself and God. Any rite, therefore, which marks a natural transition, also has to take into account that it is dealing with facets of the less conscious and less easily perceived issues of the future. A wedding, baptism or funeral may seem discernible for what it is; almost any number of simple descriptions may be made. But underlying all are more nebulous, but no less significant, factors. To work effectively in such a context ministers need a model by which to hold and interpret what may be happening. The idea of 'transition' provides such a model. The two primary historical transitions in human life are birth and death. In one we come to be; in the other we cease to be. They govern our ends, in both senses of that term—moments of existence and of significance. These two—existence and meaning—are inseparable, and are acknowledged as such through rites. When, for example, Bede described life as like a sparrow flying through a great hall, coming from the unknown and going to the unknown, he was not merely alluding to life's brevity. He was also drawing attention to the question of its meaning.[8] These ultimate boundaries of life limit both existence and meaning. They also condition the possibilities of development and growth. The initial relationship to the parents carries ineffable consequences for the child's development; the ending of death is prefigured in many moments of life.[9] These ultimate boundaries, therefore, are paradigms for proximate boundaries.

When we come face to face with such transitions, we are dealing with life's meaning for individuals and for their human contexts—family, relations, and society in general. We may consider this in terms of rites. If we acknowledge the importance of some sort of closing ritual around death and departure (and this seems widely unquestioned), what might be the forms of rites for acknowledging the proximate boundaries or transitions in life? Historically these have tended to be moments of social significance: puberty, when a child becomes a responsible member of society, or marriage, when the future is acknowledged and, although this may be overlooked, by implication the ending of the parents' life is noted. No doubt in various societies different minor rituals may be observed. Schools, for example, often have entry rituals, both official and unofficial. Less tangible cultural rituals also exist for the ageing. Each transition, however it may be marked, is characterized by hope and prospect for the future and at the same time by some little death. The rites, therefore, whatever form they take, are in touch with more than is immediately apparent on any specific occasion. When a body, such as the church, possesses powerfully specific symbols, which have an archetypal quality, then its behaviour in this field, if not highly responsible, will be surprisingly damaging to individuals and to society.[10]

Over a period of time some rites become more prominent and some less. We have already noted the way in which the informal rite of the first mortgage has appeared. Some rites also decline. We may, for example, discern a steady trend away from confirmation, which was a Christian form of puberty rite. Fewer adolescents seem to be confirmed, and there is a slight increase in the number of young adults. It is difficult to determine precisely why this is so, but the instance is illuminating. The church—at least, the Church of England—has during this period of decline in the number of adolescent confirmations been preoccupied with centralizing its liturgical life on the Eucharist and discussing rites of initiation. Having encouraged family attendance at the communion service, it has confused the 'normal' progression from Sunday School to confirmation class to participation in the Holy Communion. At the same time theological studies of baptism have exposed the anomalies in confirmation, and consequently the church seems to lack conviction about this particular rite. But this change has not come about in ecclesial isolation. It has occurred just as the idea of adolescence has become prominent in society. Physical and believed emotional maturity seems to develop earlier and there are consequential changes in social mores. Nor should we underestimate the way in which one group in a society may take up aspects of that society's confusions and uncertainties on behalf of all. Adolescents tend to be blamed for faults which do not strictly or solely belong to them.[11] Putting all this together we may observe that a rite of transition from childhood into adulthood has been diminished, not solely for reasons of theological insight, but also because of changes in the society of which the church is part. Confirmation as a rite has no social impact. There is now no obvious point of entry into adulthood. As an internal, and therefore limited, rite of the church confirmation has declined.

This example opens up an important issue for the church and for the occasional offices: who manages such transitions and their accompanying rites? The church has often believed that it controlled them. Throughout the era of Christendom the priest encouraged others to believe, and probably believed himself, that he controlled the rite and the person's destiny. But even then the church had to acknowledge that it was possible to be born and to die without a clerical ritual. And in the contemporary world it seems likely that people will increasingly choose how to manage both the proximate and the ultimate boundaries. What also seems likely, however, is that some rites — maybe as yet unfamiliar and unknown — will be developed. And if the church withdraws from this area, other agencies will arise. In the USSR, for example, it is interesting to observe how secular rituals have been created so that people may continue to handle those transitions which, prior to the revolution, were managed through the church. In style these new ways seem imitative of the old. What the sociologist may describe in terms of the decline of religious control and the creation of quasi-religious new rites, is to today's minister both an encouragement and a warning. The encouragement is that in spite of the decline in religious practice and of cultural changes which affect the church, many still possess a natural religion which seeks ritual and interpretation. The warning is against any tendency to think in terms of controlling a profound aspect of human life as a reminder that in all such rites the celebrants are the people concerned.

The idea of a transition may be taken further as a useful way of understanding the ministry which is demanded through the occasional offices. D. W. Winnicott has expounded a theory about 'transitional objects'.[12] Most parents are familiar with the doll or (more likely) the bit of rag or sheet without which a child will not settle and to which he turns for comfort when under stress. No substitute is allowed, whether an alternative doll, sweets or the mother's affection. The object is all. By using such a transitional object the child is enabled to develop an individuated stance of managing his own life. They are the means by which he can move from immature dependence on the parents to mature interdependence with them. The child can thus develop a sense of relationship without which he will be unable to function as an adult individual. To the observer this transitional object will be in itself unimportant, but to the child it is vital. When we turn to the occasional offices, which are primarily requests for ritual expression of a rite, they are illuminated if we regard them as an equivalent to the doll or rag for the child. The ritual naming of a transition constitutes an object outside oneself with which, however, one is very bound up. It can enable an adult, who is likely to be in a regressed state at, say, birth, marriage or death, to manage his way through the demands of such events for individuation and continuing social relationships.

From this perspective on the rituals of the occasional offices as transitional objects, three points may be noted. First, if the rite accompanying the transition is seen as the individual's transitional object, it becomes clear that it belongs to them and is invested with meaning by them. The discussions on rites of passage, following van Gennep, open our eyes to social functioning. But they may for the minister obliterate the dynamic aspect of the demand being made on him. These rites do not exist in a vacuum: they belong to the people involved. The minister may be used by people as part of the creation of their temporary transitional object. For the minister, therefore, a crucial question is the theological one: Is such use a legitimate function for the Christian church and for its ministers? This will be examined in a subsequent chapter. Here we merely note that this question cannot be answered by imposing a range of theological assumptions and expectations on the person who requests the ritual.

Secondly, there are inevitably going to be at least three levels of investment in the rite on the part of the applicant. One is historical in a social context. A birth, for example, is the beginnning of a new life and of changed relationships. It occurs at a point in time; it affects society; it, therefore, is marked in various fashions. Secondly, however, there are underlying psychodynamic aspects, of which those involved will be largely unaware. They will, however, appear to be persistent about things being right and proper, whatever explicit content the minister might wish to introduce. But thirdly, if we take the notion of transitional object into account, we have to add the necessarily irrational and improbable (to the minister) investment that people make. Here it is worth holding to the memory of the child's idiosyncratic behaviour, both as evidence that irrational behaviour is to be expected and as a reminder to the minister, when he is caught up in this, that it is not, however it may appear, an end in itself, but a contributory factor to a total process.

There follows, thirdly, from this one of the hardest points for any minister to appreciate: the process of the ritual is more important than the content. Christians are preoccupied with the meaning of words. They expound and argue over Scripture. They are acutely sensitive about the wording of promises and then become casuistical about the terms used. When, therefore, they are confronted by someone seeking a ritual expression of a transition in their life, ministers become agitated about the words used and the promises made. But for the applicant these are rarely the issues. The church and its minister are a resource for the expression of whatever the people wish to express. Applicants are dismayed, for example, when the funeral service proves unexpectedly unfamiliar, although the minister might consider the alternative service an improvement on the old. A further instance, which will be considered later, is the way in which an offered service of blessing for a child is felt to be unacceptable because it lacks both water (the archetypal symbol) and godparents. And, whatever words are spoken, the applicants will, if deprived of what they expect and require, often in their minds change what was offered. In one parish the vicar refused all baptisms and would only perform thanksgivings and blessings. After a period of shock and anger, the parishioners were heard to be saying that, whatever the vicar may have said, the service really was a baptism and that their children had been properly initiated. The minister is engaged in a process over which he has far less control than he might think. The words used and acts employed, although they might momentarily salve his conscience, are not as significant for the people as he might hope.

The issues facing the minister are, thus, personal and theological. The question is not how he can capitalize on these opportunities for evangelism, for teaching, or for some similarly forlorn hope. It is whether he can be involved in this aspect of common human experience as a minister of the gospel. But before addressing these questions, I turn to the third approach to developing a way of understanding the interaction of church and society.

Process and Systems

All the participants in the occasional offices experience confusion of some kind. The minister may have an idea of what his church stands for and what the latest policy guideline from the bishop or others proposes. He is also assailed in other roles than that of minister—father, husband, and naturally, another human being. He is caught between upholding the gospel and the church's discipline and at the same time an instinctive affection for ordinary people, without which he can scarcely be Christ's minister. Similar confusions are found with the applicants. They vaguely know what they want but usually cannot articulate it very clearly. Possibly only one of the couple comes about baptism or a wedding, thus expressing something about either cultural or personal expectations of the relationship between them. They, too, carry other roles, since, as has been noted, they represent more than they can know. They are trapped between doing what they feel is proper and what they instinctively feel is odd—going to the church and vicar. They feel that it is their church, but they know that in a sense, since they do not attend, it may not be. They almost certainly have residual senses of guilt and, therefore, wariness of the minister and what he may demand. And the prevailing consumer mentality by which most people live tells them that there is nothing in this world that can be acquired for nothing.

Such confusions are endemic in human relationships and, when we reflect on them, we may recognize that it is desirable that they should be, if we are to retain the richness and diversity of human existence. But at the moment of encounter, both for the minister and for the applicant, there is no opportunity for such philosophizing. Things have to be dealt with, and usually with speed. For this a framework for understanding and interpreting the encounter is valuable. We have already considered how the expectations may be viewed and how the event itself may be appreciated. We turn, therefore, to interpreting the process itself. This is larger than a one-to-one meeting. When, for example, the minister and a couple discuss the whys and wherefores of a wedding, they are not the only people involved. Each brings with him or herself a crowd of persons who continue to influence them. Some of these are known and may be discussed—the family—and many necessarily remain unknown—for example, society. The whole range cannot be understood, but it is important for the minister to be aware of it, as he tries to assist, guide, enable, and interpret. Yet they are as weighty imponderables for him as they are for the couple. He does not have superior knowledge. One way, therefore, of being able to hold to the perspective demanded by all this evidence is to work with a framework. By this means a minister may be freed from a preoccupation with the niceties of the couple's questions and can thus begin to enable them to explore the specific issues of marriage which face them. At the same time he is able to minister by providing a means of shaping the mass of confusions in which they find themselves.

Thinking of systems provides such a framework. Many facets of individual and corporate life display the same basic process: input, conversion, output. An animal, for example, takes in food, sensory perceptions and the like, converts them to sustain life, and leaves not merely waste (a by-product of the system) but the effectiveness of its existence in a particular context. An organization may be viewed in a similar fashion. A factory has a whole range of inputs—materials, personnel, enthusiasms, finance and so on—which it converts to another series of outputs. From this simple illustration two points emerge. First, most systems, although they may be simply described, are more complex than they initially seem to be. Thus, for example, the factory may easily be thought of as converting raw materials into manufactured goods, but that is not the only system that is operating. If the human throughput is overlooked, trouble is bound to result. Secondly, thinking in terms of such an open system is only a way of holding a consistent frame of reference, namely that in order to survive any enterprise has to act and react with its environment. A system cannot be conceived apart from its context in which it is set and thus the interaction is the focal point for discernment.[13]

This model is instructive when used of the occasional offices. An immediate thought may be to think of the church as the system. The input is people's confusion; the conversion is sorting it out and, when appropriate, deploying ritual resources; and the output is some sort of more fulfilled people. In such a system the minister would have a managerial role on behalf of the church, enabling people to pass through the total process. But this is a simplistic and false view, not least as an interpretation of the occasional offices. People who come for a ritual do not in one sense need the church. They are managing their own lives and will do so, whether the church is involved or not. They turn to the church not for management but for opportunity. What needs regulation is the interchange between the people concerned and the social, psychological and familial environments in which they are set. In the many interlinked strata of experience there is bound to be confusion between what is the system and what the environment. But the applicants themselves manage. The input is a series of feelings, some of which are their own and some of which seem incomprehensible. The conversion is the process by which these are sorted and interpreted, so that the people concerned may better locate themselves in life with themselves, their families, their neighbours, and, we might add, with God. The output is human beings or new human units (marriages or families) which can sustain a vision of life having some meaning for themselves and for others. The church and its ministers serve that process. They cannot control it.

Uncomfortable as this perception may be, it is fundamental as an insight into Christian ministry. For the minister it has particularly important consequences. It implies that responsibility for what happens through an occasional office does not rest with him or the church. But the pain of the confusions, the inadequacy of the experiences, and the necessarily unfulfilled nature of human life, remain with him. But through this he may, as part of his own vocation, carry an enlarged vision of what is happening and an image of God's grace and involvement in human life. That is Christian ministry. In order to perform this task, the idea of a system is a useful heuristic tool for giving the minister a point at which to latch on to the human experience of the applicant. It also enables him to enable the encounter to take place where it matters most for those who approach him. But it also, by holding to the primary notion of the church as having a task within its environment and the minister having a role in relation to that task, pushes the minister firmly towards his grasp of the grace of God, upon which his ministry ultimately rests.

Notes

1. E. Kübler-Ross, *On Death and Dying* (London, Tavistock, 1970); C. M. Parkes, *Bereavement* (Harmondsworth, Pelican, 1972); Y. Spiegel, *The Grief Process* (ET London, SCM, 1978).
2. Figures for baptisms and church attendance are published annually by the Church of England. Because of a change in definitions, only those from 1978 can be used for comparisons. The infant baptism rate per 1000 live births are 383 (1978), 365 (1980), and 347 (1982), against which may be set the following attendance rates per 1000 of the population: Sunday 27, Easter 47, Christmas 49 (1978 and 1980). The Sunday figure is for attendances, those for festivals is of communicants. [Reproduced by kind permission of the Central Board of Finance of the Church of England from the Annual Statistical Supplement to the Church of England Year Book (London, CIO Publishing, 1984)].
3. See *TPT* and Reed, *Dynamics*, both *passim*.
4. W. G. Lawrence and E. J. Miller, *The Diocese of Chelmsford: A Preliminary Study of the Organisation of Education and Training in the Context of the Task of Ministry* (London, The Tavistock Institute of Human Relations, 1973). Private circulation.
5. Reed, *Dynamics*, pp. 54ff.
6. *As You Like It*, Act 2, Scene 7.

7. E. H. Erikson, *The Young Man Luther* (London, Faber, 1959); *Childhood and Society* (Harmondsworth, Pelican, 1975), ch. 7; *Identity and the Life Cycle* (New York, Norton, 1980), ch. 2. A useful discussion of these ideas may be found conveniently in R. Stevens, *Erik Erikson* (Milton Keynes, Open University, 1983).
8. Bede, *Ecclesiastical History*, 2.13.
9. John Bowlby, *Attachment and Loss*, 3 vols. (London, Hogarth, 1969—80).
10. On the notion of an archetype, see C. G. Jung, 'The Archetypes and the Collective Unconscious', in *Collected Works* 9.1 (ET New York, Pantheon, 1959); *Man and His Symbols* (ET London, Jupiter, 1964).
11. Arthur Marwick, *British Society since 1945* (Harmondsworth, Pelican, 1982), pp. 75ff.
12. D. W. Winnicott, 'Transitional objects and transitional phenomena', in *Collected Papers: Through Paediatrics to Psycho-Analysis* (London, Tavistock, 1958). A convenient exposition of Winnicott's thinking may be found in M. Davis and D. Wallbridge, *Boundary and Space* (London, Karnac Books, 1981), especially pp. 56—81.
13. E. J. Miller and A. K. Rice, *Systems of Organisation* (London, Tavistock, 1967).

FOUR

The Priority of Grace

All aspects of the minister's work are informed by and scrutinized through the theological understanding of God, the world and himself which motivates his ministry. The everyday demands of the occasional offices generate stress and uncertainty in the minister because of their complicated nature. They also open up a range of theological issues. But just when the minister might hope for supportive certitude from his theology, he finds the ground unsure under his feet. The theological quagmire shifts: sacramental theology; the nature of God and his relationship with the world; redemption and salvation; not to mention the ecclesiological issues. It may seem unwise to enter so wide a field in so slight a volume on pastoral practice. But here, if anywhere, theological muscles must be flexed, if effective ministry is to be sustained. In this chapter, therefore, some of the issues around the nature of divine grace are examined, and in the next a specific consideration of sacramental theology is offered. Both, however, are set in the specific context of the church's ministry, and examples are derived from the occasional offices.

Whether we are dealing with the especially thorny topic of baptism and its attendant problems, or the possibly easier issues of marriage or death, one reality undergirds the theological exploration: the actual events of birth, marriage and death are boundary conditions of human life. The first and last are ultimate, and the third is proximate. The associated rites pose for the church and minister fundamental questions about the boundaries of the church and its interrelationship with the world. The way in which these human boundaries are linked with ecclesiastical boundaries often generates the anxiety which many associate with these offices and the guilt which ministers display over the way they do or do not handle them. The demands of people present threats to the identity of the church and the gospel. This matter of identity is the peg on to which we may hang the beginning of theological reflection.

Any historical survey of the rituals of the occasional offices will show how they have changed in the course of time. Baptism may be taken as an illustration. It is a key instance, since many of the discomforts about the church's ministry through these offices are focused in baptism. This rite depends for its interpretation as much upon the way in which the interaction between a church and its environment is perceived as upon any other consideration. R. W. Jenson, for example, directs attention to the way in which every reinterpretation of baptism constitutes also a reinterpretation of the church, and that, if the church is to be true to its own vocation, it must adjust its self-conception in each era. But that struggle towards each new self-conception does not derive from internally devised criteria. For the church has to articulate the believer's experience within a framework of expectation of the living Lord.[1] Interaction is the key. Marriage, as the Church of England is again discovering in its debate about second marriages, presents a similar difficulty. The words of Jesus may appear clear to some and less so to others. But most agree that the concept of marriage itself has changed since the time of Christ. A dispute, therefore, arises about what 'marriage' he and his followers twenty centuries later have in mind.[2] Death, too, has changed in its significance over the past hundred years or so, and continues to change.[3] We are, when faced with these pressures upon the boundaries by which the church tries to establish its continuing identity, not merely confronted with questions of ministry and its performance. The very instances themselves throw up questions about the nature of the body which offers that ministry and about its identity and continuing faithfulness to the gospel. These become increasingly uncomfortable in a pluralist society, with its ready drift towards relativizing positions.

Among the response to these pressures we may discern trends in the life of the church which affect our topic. Beneath many of the ecumenical explorations today lies the question of whether a pluralistic world requires a variety or plurality of churches or whether it needs one church to stand for an idealized community amid social fragmentation. Or again, with the many problems of authority which abound in the world, it is not surprising that the churches become preoccupied with authority as an issue and begin to look for simple solutions. The backlash against the movements of the 1960s is marked as much in the church as in society generally. The fundamentalisms—itself a partisan term of abuse—whether biblical, ecclesiastical or historical, become dominant in the church's life and thinking. All these affect approaches to the basic issue of the church's identity. Yet there is one more stance which is a common aspect of human behaviour and which has to be taken into account in any thinking about the church and its environment—projection.[4] This term describes the way in which individuals and groups dispose of aspects of their selves, which are disturbing or distressing, by projecting them on to others and then dealing with them there. When facing boundary issues which raise questions about the church's identity, special care is required, if we are not to project the church's problems and uncertainties on to others and then blame them. Among the 'others' who are most available for this are those who, for whatever reason, request the occasional offices. If we are to think about the theology which might illuminate and be illuminated by such a ministry, we have to take into account this danger as well as the question of the church's identity, which is the topic chiefly addressed in much contemporary discussion of the church and its ministry.[5]

The identity of Christianity is a contentious issue. Stephen Sykes has indicated the problems that afflict people when trying to think of essence or identity, but maintains that the church still has to make the attempt to discover a specific way of speaking about its diachronic unity, which is not open to obvious objection. Continuity itself is always assumed. It is indeed impossible to conceive anything that might be termed 'Christianity' which did not claim continuity with the past and particularly with the event of Jesus Christ. But once the attempt is begun, one slips either into a form of theological blinkers, which allows unaccommodating material to be ignored, or into cultural relativism, or into so wide a definition of Christianity that it embraces everything and therefore claims nothing. Sykes suggests that we enquire under what conditions Christianity might be grasped as one thing. His solution is to regard Christianity as a contested concept, which is expressed in a series of propositions. Some of these are external to experience and take the form of the basic Christian myths and stories. The other form is internal, relating to the experience of Christian people in each generation. Between the story and the experience there is a continuing and continuous interaction, from which the identity of Christianity derives.[6]

This proposal offers a way to explore applied or pastoral theology. Whereas Sykes locates the contest between the external and internal aspects of Christianity within the church, we might alternatively suggest that it is examined between the church and its environment.[7] Some, following this idea, might see the church as holding the myths and stories to which the world might bring its experiences. In the contest between them some truth might emerge for all concerned. Such a view is not wholly improbable, but it has tinges of an unattractive triumphalism, which is alien to the incarnational basis of the very story which the church is reckoned to hold. A better alternative is to examine the question in reverse. The world may be regarded as holding the external stories, myths and forms of belief, wherever these are derived from and however they may be conditioned. The church, by contrast, holds to the vitality of the inner experience of God. Thus two forms of experience are held together—general religious experience, which is exemplified in myth and story, and specific Christian experience. Such an interchange of story and experience produces a sense of the identity of Christianity, which discovers itself in the conflict, and leads to the necessity of the engagement between that Christianity and the world in which it is set. Since this engagement is inevitably interactive and not one-sided in its thrust, both triumphalism and relativism are avoided. What is more, such an approach articulates the vulnerability of the church in such a context, and, therefore, gives due credence to the vulnerability and faithfulness of God.

This generalized theory may be studied specifically through the instance of infant baptism. Baptism is a boundary event. That of an infant is associated with the liminal act of entering the world. It is also about regeneration, crossing a boundary from one world to another, or incorporation, joining one group and leaving another. Whether all this is understood and grasped by the participants is not at issue here. As a rite baptism is a function of the perceived or believed boundary of the church, which may at times align itself with a similar boundary in common human experience—that of birth. This means, however, that any theology of baptism that does not start from interaction across these boundaries will be deficient in theological and pastoral content. Baptisms are performed, and the act of doing cannot be separated from the understanding which underlies it and is developed through it. This is a double interaction between, on the one hand, the Christian story and human experience, and, on the other hand, the particular human story and Christian experience.

For the former there is ample evidence, not least in the form of liturgies. The latter view, however, may be less familiar, and for this we have to examine some of the images of baptism. These form a series of symbols, chief among which are birth and water. No baptism in any religion seems to have been without these components, and both are powerful natural symbols.[8] To these the church has at times linked other symbols—light and fire, as in the connection with the Easter vigil and the paschal fire and today in the more modest suggestion of handing the parents and godparents a lighted candle. Water, fire and light belong to the realm of archetypes. However intimately Christians tie their own specific interpretations to these symbols, their archetypal value and effect will out whenever they are invoked. So, for example, however much Christians may try to emphasize dying and rising with Christ as the basic baptismal image, they cannot eradicate the other associations, such as those of purification and uncleanness or of thirst and pure water. So if we ask whose story or myth we are handling, even in the primary Christian sacrament, we have to acknowledge that it is not exclusively Christian property.

They are the possession of human beings and are the church's on loan or by temporary, partial appropriation.

This is not easy for Christians to accept, and the problems that such an insight raises are dealt with within the church obliquely and sometimes roughly. Today, for example, baptism seems to be increasingly historicized. We are told that the church has again entered a pre-Constantinian world, that Christendom (a term of abuse) is no more, and that the life of the church is now similar—some would claim almost identical—to that in which the first Christian communities established themselves and developed their faith.[9] But a moment's reflection will expose the error. There is no sense in which the present age may be described as pre-Constantinian. Nor is there very much in common between the first and the twentieth centuries of the Common Era. And although some may delude themselves into thinking that they can experience precisely what their predecessors experienced, most know that this is not possible. All live in a post-Constantinian age which is still affected, and will be, by its response to the fact of Christendom.

A second attempt at handling the problem of baptism as a boundary sacrament is by projection. Within the Church of England, for example, we find violent disputes about baptismal practice. Groups and individuals are labelled 'indiscriminate' or 'rigorist'. It is doubtful whether there are or have been many who really baptized indiscriminately. The act of discrimination is itself qualified by the historical and cultural context in which it occurs. Equally 'rigorist', with its overtone of ungraciousness, does no justice to the pastoral intent and effort of those who appear to restrict baptism. This controversy seems to have taken over the violence from the previous dispute between paedobaptists and credobaptists. Churches may today agree among themselves to disagree for the time being about baptism, whilst within particular churches anger flares. But the argument is not primarily about the practice of baptismal administration. It is fuelled by a range of uncertainties (in spite of the many claimed certainties) about the identity of the church and the nature of its engagement with the modern world.

None of these controversies can be resolved by the usual

courts of appeal. This perception itself is a further contributory cause of the arguments. For Scripture is notoriously
unhelpful in this field. In spite of much study, which has
clarified many points, in practice the modern church is still
not much more enlightened on infant baptism than the
compilers of the Thirty-Nine Articles.[10] The church's history
and traditions compound the problem. So great is the variety
of interpretation during the first five centuries that almost
anything can be, and is, demonstrated from tradition. From
this follows the inevitable failure of the forlorn hope that
liturgiologists might rescue the church's pastoral practice.
That we know more about baptismal practice merely informs
us of the different conditions which applied at various
moments in the church's history. We are thus only prevented
from absolutizing any one practice. Indeed the major effect of
the liturgical movement in relation to the occasional offices,
especially baptism, seems to have been to provide an apparent
justification for shifting the question of the church's identity
from its boundary with the world into the private realm of its
self-defining behaviour in the other dominical sacrament, the
Eucharist. For this seems to be replacing baptism as the
point of dispute about Christian identity. The metaphor of
the Body of Christ, ritually confirmed each Sunday as people,
who know each other well, clasp hands or embrace to prove
it, and theologically emphasized through thinking about the
eucharistic community, has relegated questions about the
company of the baptized to second place. In so doing, some of
the issues of baptism are believed, somewhat complacently
but nevertheless comfortingly, to have been resolved by
default. For it is regarded as merely the mode of entry into the
community which celebrates the Eucharist.[11]
    A dilemma confronts us. Baptism may no longer be
regarded primarily as a matter of church membership.
Historical and liturgical precedents show that it carries a
wider range of meaning, and psychological insights suggest
that it remains more generally significant than this. Consequently the question of Christian identity or the church's
identity remains an acute one, which will not be resolved by
any one view of baptism being adopted To avoid this, some
might think of baptism as a sacrament of salvation from

damnation. Few, however, seem able to assign credibility to such a God and universe as is implied by this, not least in the face of the pressing, and in the contemporary world powerful, argument from experience. Oliver Quick remarks on the manifest ineffectiveness of baptism, when a baptized and an unbaptized child are compared.[12] We could add, however sadly, that this is also true of baptized adults and professing Christians. The rite does not seem believably efficacious where it matters, namely in creating or confirming a visible new quality of life in the baptized. There remains the more wide-ranging, universal view, as exemplified by F. D. Maurice:

> We tell all men, those who are most incredulous of our message, most hostile to it, that this Name is about them, that they are living, moving and having their being in it. They do not acquire this privilege by baptism, we baptise them because they have it.[13]

But even this full-blooded affirmation of the standing of all people in Christ seems only to ring bells of implicit triumphalism. These resonate with modern difficulties in understanding non-belief theologically, rather than with any coherent practice of baptism.[14]

Each of these approaches, different as they are and each with its particular merit, does not sufficiently emphasize the crucial importance of *seeing* baptism *as* a function of the church's boundary. If the rite (as with each occasional office) is viewed from this perspective, we shall necessarily and inevitably not be able to define it completely. The notion of a boundary implies continuous interaction or transaction across it. There are several theological axioms which therefore become primary for pastoral ministry, although it also follows that these will modify their context and be modified by it. Before outlining these, there is one further function of baptism to be noted and preserved in any theological reflection on it. Each occasional office is not merely a rite by means of which the church addresses the world. It also speaks at the same time to the church which performs it. For whatever else it may be, baptism is not, in its symbolic or story form, merely an expression of the Christian story. It is also an announcement or confirmation of a basic human story, which presumably has been written into mankind by God himself. The rite, therefore, cannot be done to people, but only with them, and the message conveyed or the experience interpreted is directed by God at least as much to the church as to the world.

Four theological axioms may now be discerned as fundamental for any consideration of ministry through the occasional offices—or, for that matter, any other ministry. Like any theological proposals these are bound to be controversial. This is especially so in the sensitive area of the church's ministry with those who may regard themselves as members requesting their rightful ministry but who, by any other criteria, are non-members.

The World is God's

The point is obvious, but if there is any division between mankind in general and Christians in particular at the root of thinking about ministry, then the stuff of experience with which people come to the church will be devalued and ministry will be difficult, if not impossible. Common human experience, especially in the inarticulate form that it takes around these life-cycle events, has to be valued positively as part of the divine creation. It may then form a basis upon which the meaning of the gospel may be constructed by minister and applicant alike. 'We are all immigrants in the world we now experience.'[15] The precise content of that experience lies beyond our present brief, but we may note that it is marked by two chief characteristics—alienation and isolation. Significant changes are occurring in our human relationships with our environment and within our societies. As a result, an alienation from these familiar supports has become more important than the usual Marxist sense of alienation through economic oppression.[16] There is, however, also an additional sense of isolation. In his technicized society man seems to be isolated even from the possibility of divine grace.[17] The apparently simple affirmation, therefore, that the world is God's, leads to a profound examination of what this might mean for the church's activity.

The vision of the writer of Deutero-Isaiah provides a launching-pad for this theological enterprise. He appreciates the benefits of exile—alienation and isolation—as contributing to an ultimately enlarged vision of God through a greater imagination about the world in which the natural and the political are linked. But however majestic the vision of God becomes, the writer avoids a corresponding devaluation of common human experience, not least through his interpretation of the servant of God. This perception of God cannot be restricted to the concerns of the visible people of God alone. This perspective, bold and risky as it is, may illuminate the way in which the demand for the occasional offices may be valued because it is part of common human experience. The minister is viewed as God's representative (the servant), one who enables people, through the way in which he treats them and allows them to treat him, to hold together their fragmented experience of their present existence.[18]

Christian Life is a Dialectic Existence

Mission and ministry are twin facets of Christian living. Whatever detail might be extracted from each term, they each direct attention to the obvious point that the church and the Christian life may only be discovered as it is lived with others who are not Christian. One basic means of human individuation is the growing recognition by the I of that which is Not-I. As life and maturity develop, relationships are created with this Not-I.[19] A similar process applies to institutions, of which the church is one. Without a world which is Not-Church, there could be no Church. For the church to be the church, therefore, the world must be the world. But for there to be anything, church or world, there has to be a prior creation. Both have the same origin. But God may be discerned and discovered in the interaction between the varied facets of divine creation.[20] Therefore, such interchanges as there are, for example, over the occasional offices are prime moments of potential divine revelation both for the applicant and for the church. To try to escape from this ministry, therefore, must reduce the church's capacity for an awareness of God himself and consequently for identifying itself.

Grace is Not Cheap

This theme naturally follows from the previous two. One of the dangers attending the contemporary church is that of trying to survive by projection. This manifests itself in the movement towards notions of spiritual purity and Christian identity. Double standards may result which, although sought for apparently the best of reasons, weaken the church's life and ministry. There is an instructive parallel between modern trends to general rigorism of belief and practice, including the occasional offices, and the history of early monasticism. That movement, rigorous as it was, was flawed because it implied that genuine Christianity could only be the achievement of the few. The outcome was a hunt for merit under the guise of humble dependence upon grace.[21] But if that perfection or maturity is not to be found in the compromises and problems of common human experience, then it is not likely to be discovered in precious, narcissistic groups of like-minded people. Either way, however, the question arises of who will bear the disappointment involved in ministry. It is one thing to say to those seeking the performance of a rite that the grace of God is not cheap, but that it has demands—this we shall examine in a later chapter. It is quite another, however, to inflict the cost of grace upon others because, so it implies, Christ and his disciples cannot bear it. There are moments when non-Christians seem to have to bear the pain of Christian concern with identity as sons of God. That is a curious reversal of the gospel.

The Priority of Grace

This topic takes the matter of risk a stage further. In any pastoral encounter is the church to risk its integrity and, as it might believe, the integrity of God himself? Or is the risk to be left with the applicants? The issue ultimately rests not with the teaching of any particular church, but more immediately on the judgement of the pastor. Two reflections suggest themselves. First, at the root of Christian belief is the affirmation that God has made himself known in one who is

unjustly killed to no immediately apparent effect. He is one
who bears the risk of being misunderstood and allows the
misuse of himself.[22] Second, there is the saying that those
who seek to save their lives will lose them (Matthew 16.25),
which forms the basis of discipleship. This indicates that the
true nature of divine graciousness is that, in order to affirm
others, even if they are mistaken or limited in their
understanding and appreciation of God's world, it will risk
being misunderstood, be prepared to be assigned little
significance in this life, and, when necessary, accept abuse.

These four indicated stances require considerable amplifi-
cation, which is the theological task of the minister and the
church. They are not a recipe for laissez-faire in pastoral
encounter, but they outline the parameters which for the
Christian seem to be drawn by God himself and within which
ministry is to be developed, interpreted and exercised.

Notes

1. R. W. Jenson, *Visible Words. The Interpretation and Practice of Christian Sacraments* (Philadelphia, Fortress, 1978), p. 150.
2. See, e.g., the two reports *Marriage, Divorce and the Church* (London, SPCK, 1971) and *Marriage and the Church's Task* (London, CIO, 1978).
3. G. Gorer, *Death, Grief and Mourning in Contemporary Britain* (London, Cresset, 1965).
4. The term is here used in a popularized, general sense. For a delineation of the range of uses of the word see J. Laplanche and J.-B. Pontalis, *The Language of Psycho-Analysis* (ET London, Hogarth, 1973), pp. 349ff.
5. H. Küng, *The Church* (ET London, Search Press, 1968); J. Moltmann, *The Church in the Power of the Spirit* (ET London, SCM, 1975); E. Schillebeeckx, *Ministry* (ET London, SCM, 1981).
6. S. W. Sykes, *The Identity of Christianity* (London, SPCK, 1984).
7. Wesley Carr, 'A teaching church with a collective mind', *Crucible* (1983), pp. 148ff.
8. Mary Douglas, *Natural Symbols,* rev. edn (Harmondsworth, Pelican, 1973). For a discussion of this issue as it affected the earliest Christians see G. Wagner, *Pauline Baptism and the Pagan Mysteries* (ET Edinburgh, Oliver & Boyd, 1967).

9.   A. Kee, *Constantine versus Christ: The Triumph of an Ideology* (London, SCM, 1982), and J. Moltmann, *The Church in the Power of the Spirit* (London, SCM, 1978).
10.   Article 27 of the Thirty Nine Articles of Religion.
11.   David Wright, 'The Lima report: *Baptism* and *Eucharist* compared', *Theology* 87 (1984), pp. 330ff.
12.   O. C. Quick, *The Christian Sacraments* (London, Nisbet, 1932), p. 172.
13.   F. D. Maurice, *The Conflict of Good and Evil in Our Day* (London, Smith & Elder, 1865), p. 179.
14.   K. Rahner, 'Anonymous Christians', *Theological Investigations* 5 (ET London, DLT, 1966), pp. 390ff; id., 'Atheism and Implicit Christianity', *Theological Investigations* 9 (ET London, DLT, 1972), pp. 145ff.
15.   M. Hare Duke, *Stories, Signs and Sacraments in the Emerging Church* (London, Mowbray, 1982), p. 25.
16.   Marx's use of the concept of alienation is more complex than the popular interpretation of it, which is employed for convenience here. See Nicholas Lash, *A Matter of Hope* (London, DLT, 1981), ch. 14.
17.   North, *Secular Priests*, p. 291.
18.   For further discussion of these issues see below, ch. 9 and *TPT*, *passim*.
19.   M. Klein, 'Our adult world and its roots in infancy', in *Our Adult World* (London, Heinemann, 1963), pp. 1ff; W. R. D. Fairbairn, *Psychoanalytic Studies of the Personality* (London, Tavistock, 1952); D. W. Winnicott, *The Maturational Process and the Facilitating Environment* (London, Hogarth Press, 1965).
20.   J. V. Taylor, *The Go-Between God* (London, SCM, 1972).
21.   For the history see D. J. Chitty, *The Desert a City* (Oxford, OUP, 1966). And for an interpretation see D. Bonhoeffer, *The Cost of Discipleship* (ET London, SCM, 1959), pp. 38f.
22.   J. Moltmann, *The Crucified God* (ET London, SCM, 1974).

FIVE

Christian Sacraments and the Human Life-cycle

The Christian sacraments have traditionally been regarded as specific instances of that availability of grace that has been examined in the previous chapter. It is impossible to discuss pastoral practice and the occasional offices without some examination of sacraments. Not only are these offices themselves sacramental or quasi-sacramental (the dispute over the number of sacraments is not germane), but the sacraments are one of the minister's supports and reference points in his ministry. This chapter, therefore, is not a contribution to the theology of sacraments so much as an orientation into the connection between the occasional offices and sacramental theology.

Contemporary Christianity seems to have made the Eucharist its focal point for sacramental theology. In part this is the outcome of a sustained move towards emphasizing the importance of the local congregation and assuring it of its particular identity as the people of God gathered around the Lord's table.[1] But it may also be a sign that the churches, being less sure of their interaction with their environment, are trying to develop a more powerful self-awareness from within. One result, however, is that we find the churches moving in the opposite direction to that which many people still expect of them. For the church, both ministers and members, the Eucharist is the focal sacrament, while baptism (the second dominical sacrament) is minimized into the entry rite to the eucharistic community. By contrast, however, for those who bring children for baptism, this is the main act of worship, while the Eucharist remains somewhat irrelevant and remote. This disjunction is often observable in practice when baptisms are held in the context of the parish communion. Everyone involved seems to become uncomfortable: the family, who have brought the child, feel trapped into another, alien rite for which they did not bargain; the regular worshippers seem unsure quite how to behave towards those who feel like intruders but who, they believe as Christians, must not under any circumstances be so regarded. And, like the family, the regular worshippers are also caught up in a rite for which they did not bargain, with the emphasis upon congregational participation that is a feature of most modern liturgies. When we see the church and ordinary people apparently moving on two such separate planes around the two major sacraments of the church, then some examination of what this means is required.

The theology of sacraments has to be recovered as an aspect of the examination of pastoral practice rather than one of theoretical ecclesiology. In all countries where Christianity has become the dominant religion this means facing the issue which is both pastoral and theological. This may be formulated in two inseparable questions. First, what (if any) is the legitimacy of linking Christian sacraments and the human life-cycle? And second, given the historical and cultural facts, are people brought to faith through depriving them of these rituals or not?[2] These two questions take us to the heart of the unavoidable complexities of the occasional offices: the problem of identity for professing Christians; the primacy of liturgy, and hence also ritual, in the contemporary churches; the inescapable cultural and historical contexts of the church's life and witness; and the connection between ritual and faith. But ultimately all this debate directs attention to a further, more basic question: Do the Christian sacraments belong to the Christian church? In what follows baptism will be used as material for exploring this issue.

When examined as a cultural phenomenon, baptism, or a similar rite, may be found in many religions and societies. Some may argue that Christian baptism is qualitatively different from all these and therefore is unique. But if we then resort to the customary Christian approach of studying the history of this peculiar and unique rite of Christian baptism, the question merely emerges under other guises. Although baptism appears very early in the history of

Christianity, Christians were not the first to baptize.[3] Jesus' disciples, for example, if they were baptized at all, were probably baptized only with John's baptism. One of the most striking features of this rite in the early Christian centuries is the way in which it seems to have been variously understood and practised. This observation applies to all periods, and not just to the major adjustment which followed the conversion of Constantine. In most cases the theologians who wrote the theology were the bishops who performed the rite. They were largely agreed on a few points—the forgiveness of sins, the gift of the Spirit, and the unrepeatable nature of baptism—but beyond these they spoke of the rite in their own terms. The history of baptism in the first five centuries of the Christian church is one of variety and change. When the creeds mentioned 'one baptism', this could not be interpreted to mean 'one understanding of baptism'.[4] There are two important and continuing reasons for this.

First, theology during this period was regarded as a creative enterprise. The enthusiasm for taking such risks declined, however, as the experience upon which the theologizing was done, the experience of salvation, was separated from the rite of baptism. This followed upon the second main reason for the change, namely that the social context within which the Christian church established itself by interaction, also changed.[5] The major adjustment in AD 313, when Constantine formally adopted Christianity, is often noted. Yet this was a comparatively minor event compared with the fall of the Roman empire and the invasion of the Germanic tribes. This altered dramatically the practice and understanding of baptism. It declined as the setting out moment of the Christian pilgrimage (or sometimes its completion), and more emphasis was placed, not least through the mass baptisms performed by the missionaries, on initiation into life after death and by implication into the local, social Christian culture. Another facet of sacramental theology is thus disclosed. Far from its being one of the intimate, almost private, aspects of the church's theology and practice, baptism appears as a function of the boundary conditions that exist, or are believed to exist, between the church and its environment. The sacrament itself, therefore, is also adjustable to change.

This church is not that of the theoretician but that of the practising pastor. There is no space here to pursue the argument throughout Christian history, but a little illumination may be offered. In medieval Christendom baptism of infants was the norm of social practice. It had little direct link with experience. Spiritual regeneration is fundamental, but it is also necessarily secret. The sacraments become a means to sustain this way of life. The abuses of this system lead to the reformations (a better description than the customary, and typically unificatory, term 'Reformation'). The grace of God, as experienced, again becomes prominent, but the question remains whether it is possible to have that grace without knowing it. Luther found that he had to affirm that this could be the case. Others gave different answers. But in every case the theology and practice of the sacraments were inseparable and were judged to be capable of change.[6]

In modern times a series of new factors appears. The more immediate awareness of non-Christian religions alters the perception of the missionary task. Infant death is less prevalent and the sense of original sin and the need for forgiveness decline in significance. By contrast, however, man finds himself increasingly isolated, and a number of ways of affirming man are developed. People categorize themselves and allow themselves to be labelled, as if such labels assign status. New social rituals emerge.[7] And underneath the psychotherapeutic drift of our society lies the need to sustain the illusion that man, even if he cannot know God's grace, can at least have the love and mercy of one of his fellow men.[8] To this norm the churches also conform as they emphasize the incorporation of men and women into Christ and into participation in the fellowship of the church. The rite of baptism accordingly changes, as may, for example, be seen in the new rites of the Church of England with their expressions of welcome and prevailing description of the church as a family. For all the concern about the church's self-awareness and identity in the world, its behaviour at this ritual of self-identification is highly conformist to the prevailing culture of the society in which it is set. Once more, therefore, we may note a theological and cultural pluralism coinciding around the sacrament of baptism. Appeals to

Scripture, tradition and history, as means either of validating existing practice or authenticating longed-for alternatives, will in fact only witness to the richness and variety of meaning to be found in this one Christian sacrament. They also indicate the way in which, functioning as part of the boundary between the church's task and its environment of the world, baptism is bound to change. There can be no appeal away from pastoral practice and demand to an agreed theological position. Theology is created as ministry is practised.

If there is no escape to a theoretical stance, there is also no pathway from the dilemmas of ministry through the seductive pastures of liturgy. The revival of liturgical studies has had a profound effect on the contemporary church. The particular liturgies cannot here be examined in detail, but how they have come about and some of the assumptions that they represent are important. Many, if not most, churches have revised their liturgies during the past generation.[9] On the whole they have done so in the same way. Committees were appointed to change the pattern of how people related to God. Research flourished and experts (occasionally frustrated by synods) modified and directed the functions of rituals for the good of those employing them. The slow evolution which usually accompanies change in language and ritual, was cut short.[10] This is a substantial issue and more than querulousness at the supposed or genuine inadequacies of the new services. It indicates an area of difficulty for the minister, especially when he is under stress because of his engagement with superstitions, folk-religion and half-belief. For the liturgical framework which he employs no longer resonates with the half-remembered liturgies which expressed the faintly held beliefs of those who approach him. Not only is his presenting world unfamiliar in language and detail; it is also one which has been explicitly framed without reference to them. As a result the minister is caught in a series of binds, which we may list.

1. The applicants for ministry through the occasional offices look to him as one who holds a tradition. This is on the whole a melange within the corporate, folk mind, but it is held with vigour, not least in terms of what is proper and what has

always been done. As the minister knows, that 'always' may cover anything, from what happened at a friend's church to what mother says. But the sense of tradition, however vague and inaccurate in detail, is nevertheless strong.

2. The minister, naturally, is not in fact the repository of these 'traditions'. He is the bearer of a Christian tradition, which nurtures and informs him. His ministry is concerned with negotiation between these two sorts of tradition. But for him to feel confident and competent, his own tradition has to sustain him. During a period of liturgical upheaval, not least when there is a feeling that liturgies are not evolving from worship and pastoral ministry but are arriving from somewhere other than this nub of ministry, the supports of the minister's own Christian tradition are not always effective for him.

3. As a result of this conflict of traditions, the applicants for the occasional offices do not experience the minister as a reliable bearer of a tradition. He seems less dependable than they believe he ought to be, and the people, already to some extent uncertain and guilty, become unsure of the one with whom they are dealing. This uncertainty is felt chiefly at an unconscious level of emotional life, and is not therefore amenable to rational exploration and discussion.

4. The minister in turn feels that he is himself unsure about what he ought to do, his church and tradition appearing uncertain, and unable to grasp precisely what the applicants want, since they are even less confident about him. He is, therefore, in some internal disarray and falls back on various defences. He may create certainty about the church, making it rigid rather than flexible. He may emphasize understanding at the expense of feeling. Or he may reckon that discussion is too difficult in the circumstances and salve his conscience by giving people a booklet. They in turn depart with something, even if it is only a piece of paper, but also carrying the minister's disarray in them.

5. Those who can negotiate this obstacle course, either

through profound interpretation (very few), sudden grasp of the understanding that the minister requires (some in certain social groupings), or through sheer willingness to say and do anything to achieve the required result (many), arrive at their desired end of some sort of ritual.

There is an element of caricature in this outline, but the parts of the process have often been confirmed in studies with ministers. This process, as well as the tendency to repristinization in the liturgical movements, returns us to the original question of whether the sacraments belong to the church. The phenomenon of people turning to the church like this cannot be dismissed as a remnant of Christendom in a secular world. In all but the very early generations of Christians we find sacramental religiosity among those who do not practise their religion but who cling to a religious belief that is expressed at moments in the life-cycle.[11] However this may be described, it is an issue for the church and not something to be diagnosed in the applicants and abandoned there. Yet it is no use the Christian minister resigning himself to being generally religious. He is expected to be Christian. To interpret this engagement and to sustain the minister a Christian theology of religion, and particularly of sacraments in the context of religion, is required.

If religion is viewed not as a peculiar phenomenon of its own kind but as a facet of common human experience, the Christian approach will be to place it confidently in the context of belief in God's creation. That in turn relies upon more than a notion of an original and sustaining act on God's part. It always matches creation with the idea of new creation. Without this connection any interpretation may degenerate into mere religiosity. With it, however, we are deliberately taken to the heart of the Christian gospel. For the hope of new creation in Christ is precisely what is proclaimed in the distinctively Christian emphasis upon resurrection. Thinking about creation, which has released much of the energy which has produced the scientific revolutions of our era, has been overloaded with ideas of work, rationality and order. Creation is held to be a profitable and useful activity; the world is potentially rational; and somewhere running through everything is a basic order. These ideals also dominate pastoral ministry, with its emphasis upon work and busy-ness, on the need for understanding, and the longing to impose order on what seems a chaotic experience of ministry. The religious impulse, which presents itself in the occasional offices, wishes to go further. Where there is order, there is also the disorder either of enthusiasm or of superstition, and where there is a sense of the need to work, these people bring in an almost irresponsible gaiety or play.

Resurrection, which is new creation, reminds us that all creation is an act of divine choice, whether it is making the world or raising Jesus Christ. Choice, however, is the prerogative of the leisured, those who have choosing time, and does not necessarily have anything to do with work. The story of the resurrection is redolent with play—an empty tomb, which poses a riddle; a mysterious encounter with Mary, like dressing up; the road to Emmaus, a form of blind man's buff. Angels and messages, appearances and joyous confusion mark the resurrection story as one of fun, games and play. Creation and new creation, the vision of mankind and the free play of God, meet in the resurrection, of which all man's religion may be thought of as a pale shadow.

If, then, Christianity forms links with religiosity through its central belief, it also provides the critique of it through the one event which is the prerequisite of that resurrection, the crucifixion. 'The cross tests everything.'[12] It defies simple, permanent doctrinal categorizing and stands for self-criticism. God placards himself to be scrutinized, and those around the cross, both at Calvary and through the ages, by so examining this available God find new selves or salvation. The play of God's free choice goes hand in hand with the critique of his self-denial. Nothing can be given absolute, uncritical allegiance: all is to be tested.

In this context sacraments and common human experience may be considered together. Because the sacraments have become highly significant for the church's life, they have at times become so much the church's possession that they have almost ceased to be of value. For example, in order to handle such potent symbols, the church has hedged them in with juridical questions: Who may preside? Who may participate?

When and how may they be celebrated? The ultimate example
is the concern with validity. But even this issue, which seems
internal to the church, demonstrates how a sacrament of the
resurrection, however much the church may claim it for itself,
seems to be taken from it by the critique which emanates
from the cross. Article 26 of the Thirty Nine Articles, for
example, states that the unworthiness of the minister does
not hinder the effect of the sacrament. Historically this can be
argued. Bicknell neatly suggests that Judas' ministry might
have been as effective as that of the other disciples.[13] But
today, whatever theoretical justification for such a view may
be devised, it will have little or no immediate pastoral value.
People instinctively think of efficacy as an interactive idea. It
might, for instance, be argued that any suitably qualified
doctor may treat people effectively. But individuals exercise
choice and go to the doctor whom they believe that they can
know and trust. Such knowledge and trust constitute part of
the conditions for the cure. Similarly the effectiveness of the
church's ministry is not determinable in terms of any
theoretical grace of orders or the legitimacy of the church.
There is a profound recognition that limits are imposed on
the minister's effectiveness by his believed worthiness. In
other words, his ministry is not his possession, nor that of his
church, but a product of his interrelation with others.

If thinking about the sacraments and the occasional offices
is brought into this frame of reference, we again find that
what we may presume to belong to the church and to be
offered to people, in fact already belongs to them. These
sacraments are not the church's possession, but a facet of
common human experience within God's creation, confirmed
by the new creation in the resurrection. Hence the church
took over certain existing rituals and actions—water baptism,
passover, and a shared meal. Other areas of life followed,
notably marriage and death. It put itself in the way of people
in such a way that the expression of life which the church
endorsed in these sacraments was offered the specifically
Christian critique of the cross. Just as from time to time the
resurrection has been used to obliterate the cross in Christian
theology, so, for example, during Christendom, at times the

alignment of what the church believed were its rites and what people held to be their human rituals has occurred. But the fact that this world has now passed is not a reason for abandoning the significance which the Christian gospel and the church have given to common human experience. Indeed it is impossible for the church to withdraw these rituals, because, in spite of the contemporary historical and liturgical romanticism that afflicts the church, they do not belong to the church. If, therefore, Christian ministers believe that they have to distance themselves and the church from the world in order to further mission and ministry, it is unlikely that any pulling back at this point will be seen as reasonable. For the issue is not one about preserving Christian sacraments, but about affronting human experience, which can never belong solely to the church. Indeed, the anger which will be generated—which may take the form not just of aggression but also of apathy—will inhibit almost every wish that the church may have for its gospel and for the world.

This issue is not merely pragmatic or strategic, to be tested by counting or measuring responses to the gospel in the light of different pastoral approaches. It is concerned with the theological and pastoral valuation of human life. If, therefore, the church does withdraw from this work, it will not merely affect the people among whom it ministers. It will also diminish its own grasp of a capacity for the gospel. Each time, for example, a baptism is performed, there is a message to the applicants, but also one to the church. Living in such interaction and with its attendant pains, the church is reminded that the claims of the gospel cannot be reduced to moral exhortations or subjective appeals. The 'something more', which is the mark of any theology of the grace of God, is implicit in the interaction between church and people in this rite. It may be that one 'something more' for the pluralist society might be to resist the pressures from many quarters to reductionism. This tries to make human life, which is divinely created as rich and multi-faceted, manageable within its own terms. A vision for the occasional offices is wanted which is like that of the writer to the Ephesians, from whom this term 'multi-faceted' is taken. He uses it to describe the wisdom of God (Eph. 3.10), and deliberately there extends the boundaries of the church's ministry beyond all immediate human comprehension.

To draw together this discussion of sacraments, rites and Christian theology, five points may be listed to inform theological thinking and pastoral practice.

1. Sacraments, which are inevitably linked with the occasional offices, are not specifically a Christian phenomenon. The Christian sacraments are to be understood and interpreted against this larger context and not *vice versa*. This is increasingly an insight shared by Protestant and Catholic thinkers alike, but it is not yet a basic presupposition with which ministers work.[14]

2. Sacraments are multi-faceted and not reducible to any one interpretation. When the Christian church was first forging itself in the western world, bishops and pastors were the theologians. The risk-taking in theology was remarkable and provided a means of interpreting everyday life and experience in such a way that the gospel commended itself for its realism. The theology of the sacraments today is also likely to develop among those engaged in a pastoral ministry. It will not be a secure point on to which they may fall back in the face of pastoral complexities.

3. There are three ways of viewing sacraments, which are not mutually exclusive. These are worth holding in mind as quick tests for interpreting the minister's experience as he ministers through the occasional offices: they provide a meaning for what is the case; they create something new and different; and they always refer to something other than what is immediately given. They are thus always in their richness connected with signs, symbols and life, making links between all three.

4. Sacraments have been called 'the doors to the sacred'.[15] This description, if held in the context of a theology of the resurrection as new creation and the cross as the testing point for that celebration, reminds us that the sacred is not necessarily defined either as the church or by the church.

5. If the sacraments are so regarded, we may also see that they function on the working boundary of the church in order to preserve the church from itself. The social values that they reflect may be a better indicator at times of God's will than any ecclesiastical presumptions about them.[16]

Notes

1. See especially A. G. Hebert, *Liturgy and Society* (London, Faber, 1935), pp. 207ff: 'As therefore the parish is the local unit of the Church of God, the Parish Eucharist is of necessity the central act of its life.' (p. 209). This assumption seems assumed in both the Lima and ARCIC discussions of the Eucharist.
2. D. Power, 'Editorial', *Concilium* 112 (1979), p. vii.
3. J. Martos, *Doors to the Sacred* (London, SCM, 1981), pp. 163ff.
4. The creeds themselves in part developed from a fusion of declaratory creeds and baptismal credal affirmations (i.e. practice), and, therefore, themselves encompass a range of interpretation under one formula. See J. N. D. Kelly, *Early Christian Creeds*, 3rd edn (London, Longman, 1972).
5. Robin Gill, *The Social Context of Theology* (London, Mowbray, 1975), and *Theology and Social Structure* (London, Mowbray, 1977).
6. Luther's revision of the baptismal liturgy may be traced from the translation of the medieval rite in *Das Taufbüchlein verdeutscht* (1523) to the stripping of accretions in 1526. Zwingli did likewise and, with a greater replacement of old ceremonies by new, so did Bucer. For texts and commentary see J. D. C. Fisher, *Christian Initiation· Some Early Reformed Rites of Baptism and Confirmation* (London, SPCK, 1970).
7. R. J. Bocock, *Ritual in Industrial Society* (London, George Allen & Unwin, 1974).
8. North, *Secular Priests*, p. 291.
9. For the extent of eucharistic revision alone see G. Wainwright, 'Recent eucharistic revision', in C. Jones, G. Wainwright and E. Yarnold, ed., *The Study of Liturgy* (London, SPCK, 1978), pp. 280ff.
10. Kavanagh, 'Life cycle', p. 17, quotes Robert Taft: 'The long, slow and complex evolutionary process that has always been typical of crucial human patterns, such as language and liturgy, was drastically reduced to less than two decades.' See also R. Grainger, *The Language of the Rite* (London, DLT, 1974).
11. Among the descriptions listed by D. Boroborio, 'The "Four Sacraments" of popular religiosity. A critique', *Concilium* 112 (1979), pp. 85ff, are *rites de passage* (van Gennep); the catholicism of critical moments (R. Mauss); festive catholicism (R. Pannet); sacramental

popular religiosity (R. Vidales); cultural religion of life-cycles (L. Maldonado); and the catholicism of the four seasons of life (J.-Y. Hameline). Boroborio is emphasizing that this is a universal phenomenon and not isolated to any one culture.

12. M. Luther: 'The cross puts everything to the test. Blessed is he who understands', Weimar edn V.179.31, cited, and discussed, by W. van Loewenich, *Luther's Theology of the Cross* (ET Belfast, Christian Journals, 1976).

13. E. J. Bicknell, *A Theological Introduction to the Thirty-Nine Articles of the Church of England* (London, Longmans, 1919), p. 462.

14. G. C. Berkouwer, *The Sacraments* (ET Grand Rapids, Eerdmans, 1969). Such is this agreement that there is a danger of what Paul Tillich calls 'pansacramentalism'. *The Protestant Era* (ET London, SCM, 1951), pp. 105ff.

15. So Martos, *Doors.*

16. Kavanagh, 'Life cycle events'.

PART TWO

Ministering Through the Occasional Offices

Introduction

In this section of the book we shall examine each of the three main occasional offices—baptisms, weddings, and funerals. The focus turns now to the practical issues which they raise for the minister and his ministry. This is not to imply that the theological questions are forgotten. They will be allowed to emerge from the discussion and will not, therefore, be given the prominence of starting positions. The reason for this is that every minister, however he thinks about these matters and however confused he may be by them, has finally to make a judgement about what he is to do. I have proposed that there is theological justification for the church's deliberately remaining involved with people's experience at these points in life. That now constitutes the basis upon which this exploration of pastoral practice is developed.

Each chapter has a similar shape. After a consideration of the background questions which pertain to the particular office, we shall consider how it might be handled, giving, so far as possible, practical examples. Systems, which have already been mentioned, are now used to provide the outline for considering the practice of each office, so as to give some order to the process. Inevitably a number of caveats arise, not least that, since we are dealing with human beings in their social behaviour, it is probable that the social setting of each church and parish will vary and so create different conditions for and constraints upon this ministry. These chapters, therefore, neither are, nor could be, blueprints. They merely raise practical issues which ministers at least ought to note when ministering, and suggest ways in which these might be faced. The illustrations are all drawn from actual instances of ministry, which have been offered by experienced clergy. But there is no attempt at case study in this section. The intention is to offer a framework for interpreting the everyday ministry through the occasional offices. Readers, therefore, are invited to test this approach by seeing to what extent it illuminates their current experiences of ministry.

SIX

Infant Baptism

For centuries the Christian church has baptized or christened children. The clergy of the Church of England have been required actively to encourage parents to have their new-born offspring baptized.[1] Such behaviour has not been without its critics inside, as much as outside, that church. The nineteenth century saw a major pastoral and theological upheaval over the issue. Not only were there disputes between church parties, which consolidated around the Gorham case, but several parish clergy began to feel increasingly uncomfortable with the rite.[2] Hensley Henson, when Vicar of Barking, used a University Sermon at Oxford in 1896 to condemn the modern practice as 'indecent in itself, discreditable to the Church, and highly injurious to religion'. In 1907 Roland Allen resigned as Vicar of Chalfont St Peter on the grounds of the lack of differentiation between members of the church as believers with obligations and those who felt that they had a right to belong.[3] These two examples are particularly illuminating, as neither Henson nor Allen were party men and each parish was socially different. After the Second World War similar views became more widespread among the clergy. Following debate at the Lambeth Conference (1948) and meetings of the Convocations (1942—54), an outline baptismal discipline was published in 1957.[4] But the clergy, both those who tried to observe it and those who did not, began to find that it led to conflict with their parishioners. As a result there was a number of conferences, such as the national ecumenical gathering promoted by Parish and People in 1965 and a series of diocesan events.[5]

The Diocese of Chelmsford, for example, was typical. In 1963 a residential conference of clergy almost unanimously asked the bishop to devise and promulgate a policy for the administration of infant baptism. After a synod on the theology of baptism, at which the Cambridge theologian Geoffrey Lampe gave the key paper, clergy and lay synods were established to discuss the whole question. Votes were finally taken on seven propositions, which, although the percentages for and against might have changed in the interim, remain a useful guide to the strength of feeling:

1. Holy Baptism is rightly
   administered to children   F.94%   A.6%

2. Christian parents may rightly
   postpone the baptism of their
   children until the years of
   discretion   F.51.5%   A.48.5%

3. The church should provide a
   service of Thanksgiving for and
   Blessing of a child   F.53.6%   A.46.4%

4. In present circumstances this
   service should be offered for all
   children, including those looking
   forward to baptism   F.36.6%   A.63.4%

5. Baptism should not, save in an
   emergency, be administered
   without preparation of those
   concerned   F.98.3%   A.1.7%

6. No child may be baptized
   elsewhere than in the parish in
   which the parents live, or are
   qualified as electors on the
   Electoral Roll, save with the
   consent and co-operation of the
   minister of that parish   F.87.3%   A.12.7%

7. Baptism should normally be
   administered in the presence of
   a congregation of regular
   worshippers   F.89.4% A.10.6%

[These votes were cast by a total of 1053 persons, 477 clergy
and 576 laity at three separate synods held in November
1967.]

The bishop then drew up a policy which largely embodied
these ideas and he invited the clergy to follow it.[6]
Many clergy are still willing to baptize infants. Those who
find this in conscience difficult are protected by being able to
postpone the service or offer in its place a blessing. But
correspondingly greater sophistication is demanded of the
applicant, whether in Christian commitment or in being able
to draw distinctions between the two rites of baptism and
blessing. The local congregation is widely involved in the rite,
so that baptism is less a private affair than it was. And any
potential conflict between the clergy over so sensitive a
pastoral issue is handled by the requirement that they notify
one another if a baptism is to be performed other than by the
parish priest. But the most significant figure is the nearly
hundred per cent support for preparation, which was exactly
the issue facing the Convocations in 1957. In spite of the
demands on time and energy, both clergy and laity believed
that this was a point of ministry at which intensive work
should be attempted. This is probably the most enduring
product of the debates of the 1960s. Either baptisms are
performed after preparation or they may not be performed at
all.
   But if baptism now appears in this light to the church, it
seems very different to those who seek it. Underlying the
belief that infant baptism is possible is the church's
assumption that adult baptism is the norm from which it
derives. This is emphasized in the modern liturgies.[7] The
church begins, therefore, with an assumption about itself. By
contrast, however, for most people baptism is a rite which is
performed on children, especially babies. Young children
themselves regard it as something done to babies, which is

certainly not for them. The old word 'christening' persists, in spite of the church's attempts to replace it with its own term 'baptism'. Discussions in the churches generalize about the rite and the sacrament. But in the pastoral context the striking point, as with the occasional offices in general, is that each baptism is unique. The request itself often has its own surprising rationale, which is not explained in terms of family customs or grandparental influence. For example, in urban and suburban parishes some clergy discern a move away from family tradition. Young parents seem to wish to express something about themselves and their new family, rather than merely to continue a tradition. Increased mobility disperses families. One result is that children may be presented for baptism a little later in life. The parents may have had to move away from their home area into new accommodation as soon as the child was imminent or born. By the time the second baby arrives they have settled into their new environment. They then bring both children as a token of their family having been established. This sort of observation has to be taken into account, if the minister and the applicant are to engage each other.

Since the request for baptism is peculiar to each person, the first and primary skill of the minister is that of listening carefully and hearing the coded phrases which give the clue to the point of contact. Some of these may be too quickly discounted. That a child can only inherit if baptized is obviously untrue. But the issue being raised by such a misapprehension may be that of the child's legitimate membership of family and society, when the parents are unsure of their own place within both. Another common suggestion is that a person cannot be buried in a churchyard unbaptized. And regularly put forward is the proposition that the parents wish their child eventually to be married in church. It is easy for the minister to say that none of these has anything to do with baptism, although he might recall how often the church does enquire on its forms. But each of these apparently irrelevant questions contains clues. If, for example, baptism is thought of as concerned with the beginning of life, then marriage and burial seem distant. But each of these enquiries is about the role of parents, what it

may mean to do the best for their child and how they can
create the new continuity of the new family. This may be
especially acute at the birth of the first child, but any
subsequent child also creates a disjunction in the pattern of
life. Then people are thrown up against their fundamental
beliefs, hopes and fears. One increasingly common instance
of this is reported by ministers. This is the divorced parent,
usually the mother, who wishes through this rite to state to
the child and to the world, as well as to herself, that divorce
does not represent failure as a human being and unworthiness
to be linked to society. Behind this and similar requests lies
the wish for the assurance that the child will have the benefits
of life which may have been denied to the parents.

We are now far from the discussion about the theology and
practice of baptism. At times it seems that the gap between it
and these pastoral issues cannot be bridged. One thing is
sure. If for centuries the church has insisted on the baptism
of infants, actively pursued parents to have it done, and
urged it as a duty to God and to the child, it is not possible to
reverse that teaching by a mere change of doctrinal stance.
Ministers, therefore, need to be able to hear what people are
requesting, and in order to do that they need to avoid
pressures to categorize applicants. Sometimes clergy speak
with what sounds like contempt for people's simplistic beliefs.
They are dismissed as superstitions, but without any attempt
on the minister's part to understand them pastorally or
interpret them theologically. Some translations of the word
deisidaemonestoros in Acts 17.22 may have contributed to
this. It means not 'superstitious' but 'god-fearing' or
'religiously scrupulous'. Paul used it to interpret the
Athenians' experience as a means to proclaim the Christian
gospel.[8] This problem also faces contemporary ministers:
how are they to value human beliefs and feelings, both in the
sense of acknowledging their integrity and, more intriguingly,
perceiving their status within creation? That the outcome of
this ministry will in every case be incomplete must follow
from the uniqueness of every human encounter. But such
incompleteness, although it may be discomforting, does not
invalidate the attempt. Eric James elucidated this in his
reflections on the 1965 conference, *Crisis for Baptism.* He

describes how a woman from a hostel for the homeless asked for her baby to be baptized. She had no husband and no friends, and the child had little, if any, obvious chance of being brought up in a Christian environment. Nevertheless Eric James involved some of the congregation and performed the ceremony. In so doing, he argues, the congregation and this lonely woman were reminded that they belonged to each other under God, and she was assured that her homeless, fatherless child was as valuable to God as any other.

To me the sacrament was that day proclaiming something new to the heart of the Gospel. I do not say that it is *the* Gospel. I do not say it is all of the truth of baptism; but it is part of the truth of baptism I am reluctant to surrender.[9]

The Approach

The range of possible reasons for coming to the church seeking baptism for a child is as great as the style with which the approach may be made. The type of parish or church will affect this, as will the relationship, real or presumed, of the parents to the church. The rural vicar, with the occasional baptism of a child about whose birth most, if not all, will be aware, is in a very different position from the minister on a housing estate full of young parents and many babies. The first vicar may initiate the contact, whereas the latter has no such opportunity. However, three principles underly all such encounters. First, they are personal, and are concerned with a significant event in the parents' lives. It may not be an important event—the child may not even be wanted—but it is significant. The birth may not be a joyous event, but the parent or parents often come. In one large parish, where 300 or so children are baptized each year, the vicar estimated that at least one third of these baptisms dealt with a guilty secret. The child was illegitimate or unwanted or abused. There was little joy surrounding its birth or celebration over its baptism. But the request was made. The encounter with the church is significant and, since it is a personal encounter, care has to be taken to ensure that it is felt to be just that. Second, although the applicants may believe, and even feel, that they are individuals, they also represent wider groupings than themselves and their immediate families. They will be largely unaware of this, except in so far as friends and acquaintances may be involved. But because they are also representatives within the larger society, the baptism is not, nor can it be, a private affair. Even a royal christening, which is sometimes criticized for being held in private, is not. Press coverage and publicity surround the event and few can fail to be aware that it is happening. Thirdly, unless they are regular worshippers, the parents are likely to be ignorant of the ethos, language and rituals of the church and to feel guilty about that ignorance. Their approach, therefore, will be diffident. This nervousness is often expressed by mother coming alone to make contact, a factor which requires not resistance but interpretation.

Every encounter has to be managed with these characteristics in mind. Certain practical consequences follow. First, no such approach can be treated casually. One way to emphasize the significance of any meeting is to manage it carefully. The urban vicar, therefore, who has a reliable system of being available for such requests at specific times at a particular place, conveys a message of willingness which is far clearer than that of one who claims to be available at any time, but who either is not there when someone calls or appears upset by an intrusion at an awkward moment. The word used to describe such managed availability is not unimportant. Ministers frequently advertise a 'surgery', which offers a false analogy for what they are doing. It suggests the diagnostic stance of the doctor, which is inappropriate to the church's intentions and the applicants' expectations. Occasionally clergy complain that people seem to think that baptism is merely another service provided by the National Health Service. It may not be surprising that people think like this, when clergy go to such lengths to emulate it.

Literature is widely employed by ministers during this approach phase. Whether locally produced or coming from one of the national societies or publishers, handouts are given titles like 'The Meaning of Baptism' or, more chattily, 'So You Want Your Child Baptised!'. A major assumption that lies behind the provision of such material is that people can and do read it. But even if they can be read, these leaflets underestimate the third aspect listed above—guilty ignorance. Few can understand or be expected to grasp a particular theology of baptism. Not many easily or naturally read anything at all. It may be useful to recall that even the Ethiopian eunuch, one of the few readers mentioned in the New Testament, could only manage an interesting but unfamiliar text with the aid of an interpreter (Acts 8.26ff). It is also apposite to note that, whereas many ministers complain that they lack time to read and study or that they find most books beyond them, they persist in laying this demand on their parishioners. Moreover, there is a suspicion that the number of such publications has increased in proportion to the discomfort felt about baptism on the clergy's part. Literature, therefore, seems to have become a defence for the minister's felt vulnerability. The question of written material is not one of social class—literature for the intellectual, none for the non-literate. Whoever approaches the church for baptism is expressing human feelings. These may be articulated intellectually and require some such response; they may not be, and this may demand a quite different reply. But the basic point of meeting remains personal. A handout of itself is not. A reminder of a date of a meeting, together with information about it and, maybe, the details required for the register, is different. For this constitutes an enabling invitation to continue the personal encounter established through the initial contact.

To whom is the approach made? Those seeking baptism arrive in ignorance and with a complex set of notions. Some of these have been already mentioned. In addition, however, there is the generalized idea of 'God' or 'the church'. One facet of human dependency is that such massive conglomerations can best, and for many only, be represented at the emotional, unconscious level of such encounters by a religious figure, who can be recognized and acknowledged as such.[10] Somewhere, therefore, in this approach phase the publicly authorized minister is required. In some places he will be the natural person initially to handle the meeting; in others he may, because of pressure of work and time, delegate the negotiation to a secretary or lay volunteer. There is no difficulty in this, provided that the person concerned is given the authority of a delegate and therefore is alert to what is being handled.[11] Whatever the intention of presenting the grace of God, his welcome to the prodigal, his longing to save all and his universal love—all this will crumble if it is not implicit in and discoverable through the first contact. For the applicant, therefore, a key sense is that of looking for a recognizably church person. This may be different from the keenest Christian member of a church. For what is sought is someone who can be believed to possess an adequate authority to represent that church (or God) in the mind, with which the applicant arrives. From the minister's point of view, if this person is not to be the minister himself, the issue is how he can delegate sufficient authority for the delegate to be able to act confidently in establishing the personal nature of the encounter. The minister, therefore, has here a task to perform at a stage well before that in which he becomes embroiled in questions of theology, rite and preparation.

The aim of this approach phase, therefore, is to begin the process of engagement between the applicant and the church. The chief requirement is a sense of reliability and dependability, so that the hesitations and uncertainties, which all concerned have, may be explored and interpreted in the light of the gospel. How such reliability is created will vary from context to context. But however it is attempted, it cannot be casually achieved. It requires reflection and forethought. For example, when a person enquires about baptism, a minister may warmly respond that he will call. This seems to him a friendly and reassuring stance. But even so simple an act needs thought. In the locality where this person lives, for example, who calls? In many areas a home visit implies a threat—police, rent collector, social worker, Jehovah's Witness. The prevailing idea is of someone who arrives with demand, however legitimate. In other places to call is to presume upon a relationship which has yet to be established, while in others it is a socially acceptable form of behaviour arranged through the diary. A sensitive minister will be alive to such local attitudes and devise an appropriate response. It is often important that there should be a visit, but usually not as the first encounter with the applicants. There is a seriousness about the call for them, which shows in the care with which preparations are made. But underlying all is a residual anxiety that it would somehow be wrong for the vicar to discover them as they actually are. Even in so small a matter, therefore, ministry shows itself to be something shared with people, not done to them.

However the meeting is arranged, the aim remains consistent in every circumstance—to lead people from their present position to a clearer understanding of what they are requesting. The process itself constitutes reassurance and care, and is best described as a negotiation. This rather cold word has the merit of directing attention to the parties in the meeting. The minister may not presume immediate intimacy, even though the dependency in the situation might encourage him to feel (wrongly) that he can. The applicants are assured that their ignorance is properly theirs and is not dismissed or prejudged. The negotiation is about establishing the expectations of the parents; what the possibilities are of their being realized; and whose responsibility this will be. It is a thoroughly human negotiation, in that it persistently returns to the basic stance that they are the parents and they are, therefore, responsible under God for the life of their child, whatever they may ultimately decide. It is also, therefore, important that this encounter, wherever and however it is arranged, should involve the baby itself. He or she has a legitimate interest, however small, and without this physical presence both applicants and minister may unwittingly slide into unreal areas in the negotiation.

The approach phase of the process has limited aims and one task. The task is to enable applicants and the church to establish working boundaries. This term is used not to refer to barriers of membership, who is in and who is out, nor to issues of the parents' standing in relation to the church. 'Boundary' is a notional way of describing that which between the applicants and the minister has to be neither assumed nor ignored but carefully and deliberately worked on.[12] The aims of the church are to establish this through a considerate welcome, which assures the parents that whatever they may dimly want or feel is valued for its own sake. How such boundaries are established and negotiated will affect the total ministry of the church. The mother of a new-born child is a member of the greatest freemasonry of all—mothers with prams. Any inconsistency on the part of the minister is instantly picked up and widely broadcast. To propound a public policy, therefore, as if baptisms were a kind of political manoeuvre by the church and to fail to manage the parents' approach, will leave many unhappy legacies.

Exploring the Meaning

Preparation of some kind is the distinctive development in the administration of baptism in the contemporary church. Few ministers consider baptizing children without some attempt at prior meeting with the parents and, when possible, the godparents. This preparation may range from a quick glance at the order of service, with an optimistic attempt at explaining the content, to a demanding series of meetings. Some clergy insist on regular attendance at church over a period. What is remarkable, however, is the way in which many parents, in spite of such rigorous demands, persist through to the baptismal rite, only to absent themselves until the next child is born.

This section of the chapter, however, is not entitled 'preparation', since that term has misleading implications. The prefix 'pre-' provides the clue: it refers to work done prior to the main operation. Food, for example, is prepared before it is cooked and eaten, which are the main objects. At school 'prep' is done before the main business of lessons. If this picture is used in connection with baptism, the main operation is the performance of the rite itself. It is thus not surprising if people regard that as the climax of the process and feel that their part is now over. That is not the intention of preparation, but it may be an inadvertent effect. Similarly the term, if used publicly—'Come to the preparation classes'—has more immediate overtones of the ante-natal class, which has been the parents' most recent experience of such demand. That, too, is directed to a definite end—the successful birth of the baby. So, by extension, a baptism preparation class may be assumed to lead simply to a successful baptism. The church, by focusing on preparation, may raise false expectations both in the parents and among its own members, which are bound to conflict. For the church's assumption is about life-long commitment, development and growth into adult membership. The applicants' view is different. They look for a one-off rite. The notion of preparation, therefore, is not helpful. An exploration of meaning is required, as these questions are raised in encounter between the parents and the church and its minister.

If the applicants have successfully established a relationship through the approach phase, the process may now be taken further. For this a definition of the task of this phase is essential. This will determine not only the content of what is done, but also the way in which the exploration takes place. The task of the exploration phase is to provide the parents with an opportunity to discover the significance of their request. Making this possible is genuine pastoral ministry, in the sense that the minister offers and is invited to hold on behalf of others a number of vital markers, so that they may arrive at their own orientation and understanding. In detail this procedure will vary according to context, but there are some underlying constants.

If, as has been argued, the applicants' approach is concerned with a facet of the experience of parenthood, then the exploration also focuses on those issues. New parents are generally only too happy and pleased to be invited to talk about what it is to become a parent. There is little point in expositions of the gospel or the imposition of ecclesiastical customs in the hope that these might be grasped as alternative matters of significance. That can only reinforce the ignorant guilt of the parents and leave the observer again amazed at the amount of stress they will endure for the good of their child. The alternative to such a teaching stance, however, is very often today presented as collusion with the parents around romanticized views of love and parenthood, all of which is vindicated by the church's blessing.

Neither of these approaches to ministry is adequate. Pastoring is always linked with teaching. It is not possible to do one without the other, and this congruence underlies the idea of the local minister as both pastor and teacher within his parish or area. If these two functions are held in tandem, they moderate each other. The notion of pastoring necessarily includes interpretation of what is being done and why; that of teaching is adjusted by the addition of pastoring, so that it cannot be merely reduced to the presentation of information, whether by lecture, discussion or leaflet. A quality of life as it is lived lies at the heart of teaching. This suggests that the concept of interpretation is a clearer way of considering this activity.[13]

Any exploration of the significance and meaning of parenthood requires such interlinked ideas of interpretation. If the focus is on parenthood, a teaching approach, for example, might leap directly to ideas of God's fatherhood and Christ's sonship, using a Pauline model.[14] But this deprives the parents of the one thing which is the reason for their present contact with the church. It is *their* parenthood, not God's, that is at stake. An alternative, therefore, might be to range over the experiences of parenthood as these present themselves. This in itself is another reason for having the baby somewhere nearby. Familiar thoughts include creation — the new life is a source of wonder — or love and self-giving — the cost of having the child often emerges both in terms of limitations on the parents' freedom and upon a hitherto contained relationship. Negative feelings also arise, not least with those who may be unmarried or abused and others with secrets about which they feel too guilty to speak. Facing such issues is likely to lead the parents and the pastor to one of the fundamental questions before both: is baptism a contract or a covenant?

The difference between contract and covenant is argued by most ministers in the course of their theological studies. But when it emerges in the type of exporation that is here being described, it may be seen also as an importantly human issue. One prevailing belief is that in this world you only get what you pay for and that nothing is free. When coming about a baptism, parents bring with them this incradicable belief that contractual behaviour is the norm. Everything has its *quid pro quo*. If the parents do something, then God for his part will respond by playing his role. The church often colludes with this diminishing view of God, in spite of such warnings as that of F. D. Maurice:

If you make your faith and your responsibility the
conditions of God's covenant, and not God's covenant the
warrant for your faith and your responsibility, I am greatly
afraid that you will soon believe only in yourselves.[15]

But the one thing that is in fact most obviously absent from
the newly formed relationship between parent and baby is a
contract. There is, and can be, no established *quid pro quo:*
the love, affection and upbringing of the child, whatever the
emotional gratification, are necessarily free acts of covenantal
love. This has important consequences for the exploration
phase of the process. Oliver Quick has pointed out that, while
the marriage relationship is contractual, that between parent
and child is qualitatively different. For it can have 'no
beginning or end except the beginning or end of the child's
existence'.[16]

The idea of covenant, therefore, does not spring from
specifically Christian views of God. It is implicit in the new
relationship, which is the reason for the encounter between
parents and minister. It cannot be introduced by the minister
as a theological imposition upon some neutrally valued
relationship, since it is the material for the exploration of the
significance of the parents' request, which is provided by the
parents themselves. This may be interpreted with the
assistance of the minister, whose own frame of reference is
ordered and informed by the Christian gospel. Clergy
sometimes express disappointment at the apparent lack of
response to their efforts to proclaim the covenantal love of
God. But this derives from their failure to grasp the nature of
the covenant with which they are dealing and which they are
being invited, as a privilege, to help the parents explore.

This exploration, therefore, is conducted by the applicants.
This implies that it may venture into areas which the minister
finds uncharted. His tendency may be to create an all-
embracing structured course or series of sessions (of which
he determines the number) into which parents slot. The
assembly-line image may not be lost on them. The effect is
unfortunate. Coming with a vague sense of responsibility for
the child and for this new life, the parents are in danger of
being unburdened of their glimmer of significance as soon as

they arrive. But if the work of ministry is to match the interpretation that has been outlined, the corollary is that the parents manage any meeting, not the church or its ministers. Locating control where it belongs is the first recognition of any act of ministry. A context, therefore, is required in which they can be invited to assume the responsibility which is theirs, so as to create a means of expressing, exploring and evaluating their ideas and feelings. This constitutes the creation, rather than the imposition, of a theological frame for interpreting the meaning of human existence, and especially their own. For the minister this is a dangerous and often threatening exercise. He may be confronted with areas of ignorance in himself; he may find theological ideas being developed which he had hitherto thought heretical or had never even conceived; and all demand that he responds. He may do this by emphasizing a particular view of baptism. But if so pressed, the minister might usefully recall the earlier review of what baptism has been at various times in history. It may be that a theology of baptism for a particular time and place has to be developed through the exploration carried out by parents with the local theologian, the minister. The theology of the sacraments will be enlarged as a result of this genuine engagement between the church and the applicants for baptism. Discoveries about God for both parties are implied by such an understanding.

The Rite

Part of this exploration is introducing and examining the rite itself. There is a prevalent tendency to reduce rites to rituals. Frank Wright has pointed out that ministers seem to respond well to invitations to study liturgy and its performance more than almost any other facet of their ministry. He wryly comments that the priest and Levite in the story of the Good Samaritan may well have been on their way to a liturgical conference to judge by the way they avoided pastoral matters in their haste.[17] It is easy to substitute a concern for getting the liturgy right for the rite itself. Clergy have been preoccupied with how forms of service may best be performed rather than with creating, together with the parents, suitable forms of expression for what they wish to say. In so doing the religious process of the rite may inadvertently be isolated from the underlying presence of the grace of God, for which the Christian gospel stands. Examples of this may be observed in two recent instances — the creation of alternative rites to that of baptism and the introduction of new forms of service.

Whatever the rationale behind the production of a Service of Thanksgiving and Blessing (and even more confusedly one of Naming and Blessing), it is noteworthy that this is the one occasional office for which alternative rituals are offered. There is not yet a two-tier office for marriage (although some are beginning to advocate it over the question of the marriage of divorcees) or for funerals. A study of a number of parishes and their policies suggests that the deliberate choice of such a service instead of baptism is more likely to be that of committed Christians than of the casual applicant. Even where such a service is advocated by the minister, whether as a first step for every child or as a substitute for baptism because the parents, in his judgement, cannot sincerely make the promises, the evidence is that people generally ask for baptism. The ceremony of Thanksgiving has the trappings of baptism, except for the water and the godparents. The service is held in church; the child is held by the minister; the name is often given; and a candle may be presented to the parents. The main difference, however, is that such a service is for the parents, while baptism is for the child. Indeed, Thanksgiving and Blessing may better be regarded as a replacement for the now dated ceremony of Churching, which persists only in few localities. As such its use as part of the exploration of meaning through baptism can be valuable. As a substitute for baptism, however, it chiefly functions to salve the minister's conscience. Once again, therefore, we are face to face with the perennial question of all Christian ministry: who bears the cost of painful moments and difficult experiences?

The new orders of service, which are found in several churches, offer much useful material.[18] Overall, however, they are the creations of those who believe that content is supremely important. However, this is not the case, and this perception should not surprise churchpeople. If content were so important, it is doubtful if many hymns, psalms and canticles would be sung with such vigour. The basic faults of new liturgies, which are exposed if they are used as the basis for engagement with applicants, are two. First, there is persistent assertion—'We are', 'We do'. For rituals which are to handle people's emotions, which are necessarily confused and today possibly even more so than hitherto, there are insufficient tentative expressions to be used as access points to the process of worship. This leads to either too much self-awareness and examination, thus not encouraging people to be carried by the ritual, or to none at all. The second weakness lies in the wish to say everything and, therefore, too much. For example, in the new rite for infant baptism in the Alternative Service Book, the service begins with a long introduction, which requires knowledge of salvation history. At the time of baptism there is an excluding emphasis upon the alternative family. In the opening there is mention of the church as a family, and the image becomes contentiously explicit when a child is old enough to understand. In Section 43 the child is told that through baptism it becomes part of 'a new family'. Apart from the dubious theological justification for this description of the church, it seems curious at the moment when the family of the parents and child is being experienced intensely, as they gather with their friends and supporters, to introduce the child to an alternative, and by implication competitive, family, which most will have difficulty in comprehending.[19]

Holding to the distinction between rite and ritual is one way of enabling the minister to exercise a ministry in these circumstances. The ritual may be thought of as providing the boundaries and means by which it is possible to participate in the rite. As such, therefore, ritual is expected to have its own idiom and style, which may not become ends in themselves. To engage with people in the ways that have been outlined implies careful use of the available rituals. These follow a prescribed form, and it is not open to the minister to develop a form which allows the parents to express what they wish alone. The rite is a public event and its ritual expression is one factor in keeping it so. It emphasizes the reality of the boundary between church and applicant and the negotiation which is necessary. The form of service, however, can be opened up as part of the exploration of meaning. If the things, which the parents discover that they wish to express, emerge in the course of this exploration, they can be gathered together and set alongside the order of service to see where this expresses them adequately, where it seems not to, and, most importantly, where it brings from the resources of the church's gospel and history ideas and interpretations which the parents may not possess. In the course of this activity it may be appropriate for the minister to respond to requests for something other than baptism, as these emerge from the discussion. But eagerly to offer an alternative is an escape from the work and demands of ministry. This is not a mechanical activity. It requires skilled teaching of the sort which comprises the heart of pastoral ministry.

The service is part of the total process that is being described and not an end in itself. The text may be used to link the exploration of meaning to the rite itself, the ritual of which is then an expression of that understanding. Some of these issues will have been raised during the exploration by the applicants with the minister. But baptism is a public act and a public service. This is a recently recovered emphasis.[20] There is, therefore, another component to the rite — the members of the church. They, too, need to understand their role, not merely so that they may appear competent at any service and thus serve the applicants' necessary dependency, but also so that the second aspect of the sacrament — its ministry to the church — may function. Although public baptism during the main service of the church's worship is widely advocated, this can be unreasonable in places, for example, where baptisms occur almost every Sunday. No congregation will develop its life in an atmosphere of continual baptisms. From the point of view of the ministry with the applicants, too, this arrangement is not always desirable. The modern eucharistic rites, with their congregation-centred emphasis and declaratory style, are not the most welcoming form of worship for the neophyte, even after explanation. Each church will have its conditions and develop its own way of coping, but all have to enquire about the task of this phase in the baptismal process.

The main service of the church may stand for the gathering of Christian people, or it may merely appear to be another ritual in which the applicants are required to participate. There are ways of expressing the involvement of the congregation in baptism without requiring this to be indicated through one particular form of liturgy. Indeed, it would appear to be an extraordinarily limited group of Christians that could only worship in one way. If the church insists on baptisms at, say, 9.30 a.m. on a Sunday morning, without taking into account mobility and family movement, it will not be surprising if its worship, far from being a boundary across which people can move to discover significance in life, will become a barrier to all but the most resilient. There is no reason to leave all this exploration to the parents. The Christian congregation may also be taught about the responsibilities and demands of the baptismal life-style, which they are authorized by their own baptism to exemplify. This includes sharing other people's experience at some expense to one's own time. For this to be effective, however, the task to be performed has clearly to be understood. Members of the congregation are not asked to be present; they are required to be partners with the minister in the carefully prepared process of baptism, particularly at the ritual phase. In this way the sacrament is liberated to serve parents and child, minister and congregation alike.

The baptismal rite is heavily loaded with symbols, which do not of themselves belong to the church. The minister's task in ordering the service cannot be performed, if he merely indulges his predilections. He is acting on behalf of a range of people, using powerful symbols which, because of their very nature, he cannot control. His own ministry in this field, therefore, requires constant scrutiny, both from the feed-back which comes from others and that which he finds in himself. For he will develop and adjust the ritual as he performs it over the years. Religious symbols are powerful, but from time to time they lose their potency. For example, among the symbols which at various times have been associated with

Christian baptism, have been the sign of the cross, light, a white robe, immersion, anointing, breath, the dove, fire, light, and, of course, water (although even this apparently simple ingredient can prove more complicated than it sounds — hot or cold, running or still).[21] Around each of these is a heap of associations, some natural and primitive and others conditioned by Christian culture. The minister may too easily be locked into the latter. Thus, for example, Michael Perham comments that baptism is '*most obviously* about healing and wholeness'.[22] However true this may or may not be, it is not obviously so. Today's trends to the repristinization of liturgical activity may, if not handled with care, divorce the minister from the material of the process of ministry in which he is engaged. All aspects of the ritual, therefore, need regular scrutiny.

A specific example may be taken from the giving of the lighted candle. To the Christian this may be a sign of the light of Christ, as the baptismal candle is lighted from the paschal candle, which itself is sited near the font. The whole ceremony is redolent with powerful symbolism, which has been endorsed by the Christian church. But some parents exhibit discomfort at receiving the candle, not knowing what to do with it, and finally extinguishing it. For them the light of life applies less to Christ than to the infant, and it is this newborn, precious life which appears to be snuffed out ceremonially. Instead of bringing people through dimly held beliefs into a glimpse of the light of the gospel, the casual use of this symbol may plunge them further back into superstition. It is also observable that this occurs as much with church members, who bring their children for baptism, as for anyone. The way for a minister to avoid such pitfalls and minister as effectively as he might in such circumstances is through careful reflection on his experience and, so far as he can, on what he sees of the applicants. He may then adjust the ritual, less in the light of new liturgical insights, useful as these sometimes prove, than as people appear to make use of the rich, multi-valent symbolism of the rite.

Feed-back

The final phase of the process is feed-back. This term is preferable to the more customary 'follow-up', since it reminds the minister again that, whatever his contribution to the process, he is part of it. He does not control what happens.

It is unlikely that there will be very much direct feed-back from those whose children the minister baptizes. The mobility of people means that it is more probable that he will pick up responses to the ministry of others. He is, therefore, caught up both in a network of pastoral practice, of which he will be unaware in any detail, and of people's lives on which other ministers and churches have at various times impinged. This rather vague material, often communicated in feelings and unconscious behaviour, constitutes feed-back. A variety of approaches to local follow-up of baptismal contacts has been attempted: visiting, a cradle-roll, cards delivered by members of the church (often the Mothers' Union), attempts to link mothers with women's groups, street wardens, and invitations to anniversary services. Behind all these, however, remains the assumption that the baptism of the child was an event between the family and the church. But the parents represent more than this, and the church, too, is larger than its own self-awareness. Any one-to-one contact, therefore, will be loaded with other concerns of the church, much to the parents' mystification and to the despair of the church members. Such misunderstanding is not helpful to future pastoral work and at worst it may produce the sort of despair which typifies reports on such enterprises.[23]

If, however, the focus of the whole process is seen to be the rite itself, then the feed-back will be more diverse and diffuse than the minister and his congregational colleagues might hope. It is also, therefore, less personally gratifying. This generic problem in ministry through the occasional offices is discussed below. Feed-back occurs through the normal pastoral ministry that continues, and the test of baptismal ministry will be the extent to which the model of ministry as interpretation is sustained and allowed in other contexts and through other opportunities. One priest remarked that it was almost uncanny how often his next contact with a family after a baptism was through the funeral of a grandparent of the child. The continuing ministry of the church will depend on the extent to which people, in however general a fashion, can discern coherent involvement and interpretation of their lives through fleeting contacts with the churches and their ministers.

Notes

1. See the opening rubric to the BCP rite of Public Baptism of Infants.
2. P. J. Jagger, *Clouded Witness: Initiation in the Church of England in the Mid-Victorian Period* (Pennsylvania, Pickhurst, 1982).
3. Henson, cited in C. E. Pocknee, *Infant Baptism Yesterday and Today* (Oxford, Mowbray, 1966), pp. 1f. Roland Allen, 'To the parishioners of Chalfont St Peter', in D. Paton and C. H. Long, ed., *The Compulsion of the Spirit. A Roland Allen Reader* (Grand Rapids, Eerdmans; and Cincinnati, Forward Movement Press, 1983), pp. 126ff.
4. *Holy Baptism, Confirmation and the Communicant Life* (London, SPCK, 1957).
5. Basil Moss, ed., *Crisis for Baptism* (London, SCM, 1965).
6. Gordon Hewitt, *A History of the Diocese of Chelmsford* (Chelmsford, The Diocesan Board of Finance, 1984), pp. 179ff. Canon Hewitt also produced for the diocesan debate a survey of official reports (1940–59) on the administration of Holy Baptism in the Church of England. I am also grateful to him for the references in note 3 above.
7. P. J. Jagger, *Christian Initiation, 1552–1969* (London, SPCK, 1970). For recent Roman Catholic thinking see J. D. Crichton, *Christian Celebration: The Sacraments* (London, Chapman, 1973), pp. 29ff.
8. P. J. Koets, *Deisidaemonia: A Contribution to the Knowledge of Religious Terminology in Greek* (Purmerend, J. Muusses, 1929).
9. Eric James, 'Reflections on the conference', in Moss, *Crisis*, p. 138.
10. *TPT*, pp. 37ff; Reed, *Dynamics*, pp. 169ff.
11. A. K. Rice, *The Enterprise and its Environment* (London, Tavistock, 1963), pp. 230ff. *TPT*, pp. 53ff.
12. Miller and Rice, *Systems*, pp. 262ff. *TPT*, p. 39.
13. *TPT*, pp. 48ff.
14. Quick, *Sacraments*, p. 167.
15. F. D. Maurice, *Prophets and Kings of the Old Testament* (London, Macmillan, 1870), p. 216.
16. Quick, *Sacraments*, p. 167.
17. Frank Wright, *The Pastoral Nature of Ministry* (London, SCM, 1980), p. 4.

18. For commentaries and suggestions for using these services see *The Alternative Service Book: A Commentary by the Liturgical Commission* (London, CIO, 1980); Michael Perham, *Liturgy Pastoral and Parochial* (London, SPCK, 1984).
19. E. de Waal, 'The changing Anglican attitude towards the family', *Crucible* (1982), pp. 106ff. The modern church seems to have acted casually in assuming the model of the family for its own life. There is surprisingly little scriptural warrant for it; the pastoral consequences seem ill-considered; and in view of the problematic status of the family in contemporary society, the negative facets of family life should not be so cavalierly dismissed in the name of bonhomie. For a criticism of church assumptions see C. A. Lewis, 'The idea of the Church in the parish communion', *Crucible* (1982), pp. 114ff.
20. Although this was reinforced by rubric in 1662, it has recently become a major issue in the Church of England. See canon B21.
21. *Didache* 7.
22. Perham, *Liturgy*, p. 7. My italics.
23. Moss, *Crisis*, p. 161, referring to a study from the Diocese of Sheffield.

SEVEN

Weddings

Baptism proves complicated for the church, largely because of the confluence of sacramental theology and a rite of common human experience. Weddings, however, bring problems for the reverse reason. Although some use the word 'sacrament' of marriage, few doubt that the couple themselves are the ministers and not the church or the clergy. But it does not follow from this that the couple contemplating marriage may do whatever they wish. Around marriage today there is a range of questions which are generated by changes both in society and in the understanding of its institutions, as well as in the psychological interpretation of persons. Books and reports abound.[1] Marriage is problematic, however, primarily because of the way that social and personal changes coincide in it.

Marriage is a social institution. The law has a deep and legitimate interest in it. The Christian connection is secondary to its being a human institution. Most customs, for example, are pre-Christian in origin—the ring, presents, groomsmen and bridesmaids, and much of the ceremonial that marks a modern wedding, whether in a church or a registry office.[2] Today's discussions and concerns about marriage and the family are implicitly about the nature of our society and its future. The question 'Whither marriage?' is less about the couple than about the sort of society that is envisaged, hoped for and being created. The wealth of sociological analysis, anthropological comparison and political intention that is generated around marriage finally issues in the couple as they sit with the vicar in a specific parish discussing their wedding. Their apparently simple relationship—boy meets girl—is set within a maelstrom of profound uncertainty and unsureness. It is, therefore, to be expected that they will to some extent feel this in themselves, even if, as is most likely, they will not be able to articulate the feelings.

Marriage is highly personal. The union of two people possesses almost more privacy in our society than the life of the individual. Governments and others are wary of intruding upon that privacy. Linked with this is the major change, whereby marriage is less understood as a contract and more in terms of a personal relationship. Feelings, expectations and the wish for growth and fulfilment play prominent parts in the modern marriage. These aspects have become even more significant since the sexual revolution of the 1960s and 1970s. The personal intimacy of sexual intercourse, to which marriage was for most the gateway, has now become less secret. One outcome is that the private world of marriage is less sexual but more personal, with higher expectations of personal satisfaction, which are, however, less definable.[3] Much, therefore, is invested in marriage, and whether this makes for a more or less stable institution may be debatable. For the minister, however, awareness of these phenomena is vital as he meets the couple who are considering marriage. With so varied a range of presuppositions aggregating in marriage, the minister will more than probably find that he lives in a different assumptive world from that of the couple.

Somewhere between the overarching social expectations of the institution of marriage and the inflated personal investment of the couple lies the reality of the two who wish to marry. But the pair, too, has to be conceived as more than the sum of the personal, familial or social expectations. It generates its own dynamic. In any social context or group the couple stands for considerable power and consequently is more of a threat than is sometimes recognized. Any pairing stands for investment, both by the couple and others, in a hoped for future. This is the case even with the most transitory of pairs, and is more so in any pair which publicly announces its intention of remaining together for a long period.[4] At the same time such a pair can also be destructive. 'Two's company; three's a crowd' is an accurate description of common experience, with its implication that the way in which a couple functions excludes others. In society such pairing is institutionalized in marriage, which is therefore not surprisingly a highly regarded activity (93% of people get married), but one which contains deep anxieties (30% of marriages end in divorce).[5] Over half the marriages in England are solemnized in a church. The figure is necessarily approximate, since the churches have differing attitudes towards performing second marriages.[6] The reasons for these church weddings sometimes seem superficial—flowers, space, photographs and music. Whatever value, however, is assigned to these, underlying them are deeper issues for the church and its ministers. The questions may be many, but the public joining of a pair with the intention of creating a new entity—a marriage—remains a significant action in contemporary society.

Marriage is more than a social requirement. Cohabitation is more widely acceptable than it was. Some figures suggest that about 20% of those who marry for the first time are living together, and that 60% of those marrying for the second occasion have already lived with their partner.[7] Personal relationships of profound intimacy are not confined to marriage. But this new-found tolerance is not acquired without corresponding uncertainties, and it may be that the church is being used not to endorse one stance or the other on such issues, but to hold the two in uncomfortable tension, while people sort themselves out. The Church of England, for example, is making heavy weather over the marriage of divorcees. Reports, synodical debates, procedural disputes, episcopal dissociation, have all marked an argument that has continued for many years. The outcome (1984) is not yet settled, and resolution looks improbable. Although the battle is fought on grounds of Scripture and tradition, it seems more likely that one reason why the church cannot settle the matter is because, as a body involved with people at their most dependent and carrying the expectations of a confused society that there is an answer, it is in a position from which it will not be able to extricate itself. The church expresses this difficulty on behalf of society but uses its own language of compassion while supporting an ideal of marriage.[8] Its error may be that it thinks this language actually circumscribes an issue which is more subtle than it cares to acknowledge. The topic has been discussed elsewhere.[9] Here it is mentioned as the background to pastoral practice. Yet 'background' itself is not a helpful concept in such an examination. What is in question is the context of this ministry. The minister and the couples will be working not against a background of these larger phenomena but with them, and specifically as these are found within the particular couple and their engagement with the church. The ministry through this occasional office, therefore, will be one contribution to the way church and society may struggle to whatever new understanding is applicable and desired.

The minister contemplating this ministry holds the larger social context of marriage as this focuses in each couple. There is also the contemporary expectation of marriage as a personal relationship, which can be reduced neither to an economic contract nor to permission for sexual activity. Such factors themselves emphasize that the key to the process is that the couple are the ministers of the sacrament and creators of the new entity. The church's ministry is concerned with human beings as human beings. The phrase 'Christian marriage' sometimes occurs. Those who are practising Christians might wish to consider the way in which the dimension of their joint faith may illuminate the human experience of marriage. But any suggestion that there is a marriage which is differentiated by being 'Christian', as compared with any other sort, is theologically and pastorally at fault. As the Book of Common Prayer describes it, marriage is 'to be honourable among all men'. This implies that what God means marriage to be may be perceived in any marriage, whatever the particular beliefs of the partners.[10]

There is, therefore, every reason for Christian ministers and churches to remain open for people to explore the significance of marriage, of their relationship, and of the intention expressed through the rite. For the rite conveys its own message to people, not least that marriage is a public act of divinely created beings, which, even when most marred and apparently deficient, has something to do with God's intentions.

The Approach

The minister may conduct hundreds of weddings each year, but every one is unique for the couple. A church office, a secretary or a verger is sometimes the first point of contact. Such personnel require induction into the style of working that is to characterize the church's ministry at this point. The most exposed person in any organization is the one who specially needs to know the task and the style of the institution that he or she is representing. A crucial notion, which all involved in the approach phase need to grasp, is that the couple are not the ministers of the rite in an ideal sense, but that they actually have to be. They, therefore, have to be encouraged consistently to take their responsibility. Anyone who deprives them of this, albeit for the best of apparent reasons, undermines the church's ministry with the pair.

Couples approach the church in a variety of emotional states, which may be summarized as 'disarray'. The step of coming to book a wedding is often the first joint act that the couple perform where their behaviour and intentions become public to a person in authority whom they do not know. Hitherto they have been involved with friends, those with whom they work, possibly the jeweller, and their families. To these they can relate without too much difficulty, because they have some idea of the assumptions that are being made about them. This is even true of any meeting with a doctor or lawyer. To book the wedding, however, puts their proposed relationship in a new light. Nervousness and anxiety may, therefore, seem disproportionate to the act. They are also approaching a church about which they will have some fantasies.[11] Today, for example, the chances are that the couple may be living together. A reason for marrying may be either the imminence of a child or the wish to start a family legitimately. Questions of sexual behaviour have probably been faced long ago. But fantasies remain strong about the church and its attitude to sexual morality. Clergy often report a general sense of nervous guilt on the couple's part, which makes it difficult for them to express what they wish to request or to engage in a serious conversation with a stranger, especially a vicar. The woman may be pregnant, and some primitive feelings of uncleanness or even wrong may be present. The man may have been able to appear proud of his virility with his colleagues, but this seems less wise a stance in front of a clergyman.

A further range of pressures derives from the family, which may contain members of different generations and a variety of assumptions about marriage. A number of studies have shown that marriage, both as an institution and in the form that people's expectation of it take, is changing, and that it is different from what it has been in recent generations.[12] The idea of marriage remains constant, but the word shrouds the differences. What, for example, seems to the family another step in the generations, with the implication that the marriage will lead to children, may be to the couple a powerfully counter cultural act. In coming to church they may be meeting expectations of doing what is proper, but at the same time by doing something which is in fact unusual, they may be creating widespread unease. An unsuspected contributor to this may be television. For this enables people to believe that they have lived aspects of life and had experiences before they themselves can have them. The actual experience then takes on an aura of *déjà vu*.[13] Put together these many factors contribute to a sense of incomprehensible conflict, which is often found around a wedding: parents, and especially grandparents, think of marriage as a new state, which cannot be experienced until it is reached; but the couple may reckon that they already know, through actual and believed experience, about this state, so that the wedding is a ratification of what already exists. And the whole mélange is compounded with the set of models that is already built into each partner, which derive from their close, often unconscious, observation of their parents' marriages.

In the light of this the sensitive minister may be wary during this approach phase of inviting the couple to join groups or intimate discussions with other couples, whether contemporaries or older. That may well be appropriate later. At this stage the task is more limited: to begin the process of enabling the couple to become publicly responsible for their relationship and their marriage. To do this they may need assistance in opening up and exploring their anxieties, whether these take the form of hopes or fears. That constitutes the bulk of the exploration. But for them to move to that position, some technical points need efficient handling during this phase. The law on marriage is strict and the minister has a professional duty to be sure about it. In most instances there is no problem, but the signs which warn of potential alarms should be deliberately checked at this stage. Among the obvious signals are whether a person has been divorced, which matters both for the law (in order to avoid bigamy) and for some churches. Age is another question. Non-British nationality requires careful attention. There is also the time scale for reading the banns and, if necessary, procuring the licence.[14]

Other less obviously technical matters arise. They may appear trivial to the minister, but loom large to the couple. For example, arrangements for a reception often dictate other requirements. The minister has to be clear about dates and times. Confirmation in writing may seem burdensome, but is normal, and sensible, practice in business. The couple may also have questions about protocol with which the minister can help. But he needs to take care lest he begins, from the best of motives, to collude with their expectations and be made into an expert on things about which he can have no knowledge.[15]

Some advocate leaving these matters until a marriage interview or preparation meeting. This seems unwise. Marriage preparation is concerned more with serious issues and should operate in an area of greater profundity than merely removing technical problems. If the minor anxieties of the couple (which may feel major to them) are not dealt with at this early opportunity, the assurance that could be theirs may be missing from later engagements with the church and its ministers. As he invites people to assume responsibility for their affairs as mature human beings, the minister is obliged to assist them in discovering what it is that they are managing.

Exploring the Meaning

In his work on marital counselling Dr Jack Dominian has outlined five dimensions for every marriage.[16] Not all will necessarily be handled competently, but account has to be taken of each. These are: social, intellectual, spiritual, sexual and emotional. Some sense of the new social unit being created and appreciation of the roles which depend on it is required, together with some compatibility between intellectual gifts and a shared sense of values. Although no longer so much something to which to look forward, sex is today considered a barometer for what is valued or lacking in a couple's life, and the mention of the emotional facet directs attention to the contemporary approach to marriage as an enriching human relationship. The minister could usefully take this framework for exploring the meaning of marriage in his ministry through this occasional office. Each area is one in which each partner has to take responsibility individually and in which shared developments must occur. But these are not headings to be imposed as a check list. Once again, what the minister holds within himself to give shape to his work with the couple, is the key factor in exploring the meaning of marriage with those about to embark on it.

There is a contemporary vogue for training, with which the church colludes. Any problem, so it is believed, may be resolved, provided sufficient training is offered. But training is a dispiriting notion with which to confront those seeking to acknowledge publicly through marriage their relationship of mutual affection and love. It also implies that there is information or a technique which can be supplied by some who have it to those who lack. But such a feeling is the last that a couple facing this new enterprise need engendered in them. Training for marriage, therefore, is not a useful model for the church's ministry at this juncture. But because the church is involved in weddings, it believes that it should offer some form of marriage preparation. This may be true, but it has to be noted that it is impossible adequately to handle in depth a lifetime's beliefs and observations, not to mention personal feelings and attitudes, during the pressured time that is available to couples between the moment that they approach the church for a service and the wedding itself. If the minister and the church are seriously to consider preparation for marriage, then this has to be part of a long-term programme of contributing to schools and other groups, not to mention its political involvement in national and local programmes.

That said, however, the couple coming for a wedding might reasonably expect their relationship and their expectations of it to stand some scrutiny from each other with the help of the minister. Marriage preparation is widely discussed at present. It ranges from extensive courses to a brief interview with the minister in his study. What is done locally will depend upon a series of factors, such as the culture and its norms and the number of weddings in which the minister is occupied. In order, however, to explore their relationship and the significance of their intention to marry the couple need certain opportunities. Among these, although this is usually overlooked, is a chance to talk separately with the minister. If the church colludes with the assumption that engagements are virtually sacrosanct, it should not appear amazed when marriages fail. Ministers tend to dote on the couple and affirm it as an already existent unit. But however intimate the couple may be, there remains a transition through public ritual to a new status. A range of responses have brought them to this point. If, however, they are to have a chance to act responsibly, a brief time for each to examine alone with the minister his or her personal expectations and motivations could be valuable and advisable.

The suggestion here being made is of interviews between the minister and the couple, both separately and together. Some parishes have inaugurated courses and group work. But however sophisticated this is, it is not a sufficient replacement for a discussion between the church's minister and those who are to be the ministers of the wedding. For the focus of this meeting is in a sense ministry: what rite they will solemnize; how this illuminates their relationship; and how this may provide a basis for continuing—hopefully life-long—scrutiny and support. The relationship which the two have already created and from which the marriage is to grow, is not something which may casually be assumed to be material for group discussion. Marriage preparation groups are sometimes offered as if they were compulsory. The value of some such meeting is widely attested, and often couples come to appreciate diligent work with them along with other couples. But such learning depends upon the couple consenting (almost, we might say, contracting) to take part. Attendance at such meetings cannot become a precondition for eligibility to be married in church. Indeed, nothing can be, since eligible couples have the right to be married in their parish church in England. Therefore any exploration of the meaning of the rite has to be mutually agreed between the minister and the couple. This legality underlines a more important dynamic point. Marriage is a private relationship, which is lived publicly and socially. The boundary between the private world of the couple and the public world, of which they are part, is extremely sensitive. It is also important that it is examined, if the marriage is to mature. Just as the personal boundary of the individual is constitutive of his or her individuality, so this new boundary performs a similar function for the marriage. Penetration of such boundaries without informed consent is morally wrong, in addition to being educationally disabling. People, therefore, have to be invited into contexts where they may of their own volition explore the nature and significance of such intimate boundaries, and not where they may find them unexpectedly under stress or attack. The interview with the minister is an opportunity for such reinforcement of individuality and value. If interviews are held with each party to the marriage, it is possible to encourage each to examine his or her motivation and attitudes without the constraining presence of the other. They are thus free for a brief moment at a crucial juncture in their lives from living up to the expectations that they have generated in each other. Very occasionally one partner may admit that the proposed marriage is a mistake. In that case the pastor's role changes and he may have to spend time in discovering what this admission implies and whether disengagement is appropriate. The whole enterprise, however, whatever the outcome, demands time and organization. This is difficult, but not impossible. And the priority assigned to this work by the minister will indicate both to the couple and to the minister himself, not to mention the church as a whole, the seriousness with which marriage is regarded.

Whether or not separate interviews are possible, there is no question about an interview with the couple. This concentrates upon the nature of their relationship and how they might try and express it, the wider significance of human love, and the resources available within them and to them to enable their marriage to grow. It is also an occasion for fostering by interpretation the notion of and need for communication between each of them. One area, however, which is often avoided by mutual consent, is that of conflict and its value. It is sometimes raised, if the phrase 'forsaking all others' is examined in any depth. Competent handling of conflict is a major factor in emotional maturing and is one for which couples in contemporary culture seem least prepared. To discuss this question, however, reminds the couple of the realities of the step that they are about to take. The minister will particularly assist by representing to them the public context within which they will be establishing their marriage. He may be able to hold on their behalf the idea of a transition that requires some management. This will also help him clarify a difference between his own public ministry and marital counselling. Those to be married come into contact with a wide range of experts, who all claim to know what should be done—parents, florists, caterers, doctors, car hire firms, and so on—and cannot proceed without them. But the church, which reminds the couple that they and no one else is responsible for them, is not another such expert. It may, by avoiding the trap of behaving as one, then provide a valuable holding environment within which the couple, both as an entity and as individuals, may find during a time of stress and disarray the momentary space to take up their public and private roles.[17]

During the 1950s churches began to provide informative courses for those about to be married. They customarily comprised sessions for a group of couples, at which practical advice would be offered. People like estate agents, bank managers, doctors and priests would take part. Some, however, increasingly feel that such courses are neither desirable nor necessary. If marriage is regarded as a relationship which is expected to develop, then opportunities are needed to examine the nature of such a relationship and its potential. The Roman Catholic Marriage Advisory Council, for example, offers such a programme.[18] If no such course is available, local bodies, such as the Marriage Guidance Council, are usually willing to assist ministers in creating one. Much, however, seems to depend upon the sophistication of those involved. In some parishes ministers point out that social customs do not include discussion, least of all on private life. They also note that the provision of basic information in a course is still valuable and may constitute an entry to larger issues, not least where the roles of the partners are highly stereotyped. For example, a woman who has never had to manage a housekeeping budget, but is expected at marriage to be able to do so, may be relieved to find others in the same predicament. And on that base may be erected a structure for examining the expectations that the partners have of each other and the reasons for them.

In each of these areas judgement has to be made in the light of the minister's perception of how the task of exploring meaning may best be performed. The aim, however, in each case remains consistently simple: to enable the couple, separately and together, to comprehend what they already know of themselves and of each other, so that they may confidently undertake the rite of marrying each other.

The Rite

The key to interpreting a wedding is to recognize that the couple are the officiants and that the minister facilitates their ministry and blesses it. Any theology of marriage which is expressed liturgically, therefore, will primarily be one which expounds the human institution of marriage and illuminates its divine facets by means of the Christian gospel. In the Anglican tradition this accounts for the fact that the marriage rite has, as Geoffrey Cuming points out, 'been more gently revised than any other'.[19] Since this is a human rite, it will not change very much in the light of liturgical discoveries, but will mildly develop as that which people need to express alters. A small example may be seen in the way in which the custom of the man giving the woman a ring has been changed to that of giving and receiving a ring on the part of each, which has now been liturgically legitimized.

Since the couple are the ministers, they have responsibility for the ritual and its performance. This is sometimes forgotten by clergy, not least in their wish to avoid disputes and, on occasion, to pacify church officers, vergers and, in particular, organists. Michael Perham reminds the minister that he is not the arbiter of taste, but that 'the chief pastoral need is to help them to relax and to feel assured that the service is in safe hands'.[20] This is true, but the safe hands are, so far as possible, first those of the couple. It follows that, although sometimes families may be invited to participate, the working relationship is between the couple and the church through the minister. The service, as part of the process, can be discussed during the final stages of exploring the meaning of marriage, and the liturgy may be used as a check against which the couple's reflections and aspirations can be tested. If it appears to express something that they do not wish to acknowledge for themselves, then there is a matter requiring study, since this probably indicates an unresolved issue between or around the couple. It does not, however, in the outcome necessarily follow that the liturgy remains unaltered. There is a wide variety of options available in such modern service books as the Alternative Service Book of the Church of England.

Details of how to manage a wedding are available in various manuals. One major stance, however, is worth the minister's attention. Marriage as an instance of mutual self-giving and personal relationship is now expressed in the modern liturgies. Its public significance, however, is less apparent. In the rite the minister's presence is a reminder of God's intention for the couple and for his whole creation. In a sense, therefore, he stands especially for the social implications of the marriage at a point where the personal investment is felt most keenly. An incumbent, as registrar, has to occupy this place legally by having to ensure that the correct procedures are followed. But his task is also to enlarge the significance of that love which is exemplified in the couple, however adequately or inadequately. *Ubi caritas et amor, Deus ibi est.* God's love is wider than the love expressed in this one instance, yet for a moment this one instance also encapsulates that wideness and divine generosity. If this aspect is missing from the wedding, the rite is deficient. The couple cannot be expected to hold such a perspective unaided. The minister, therefore, incorporates this stance in the frame of reference which he provides. In devising the ritual with the couple, he will introduce ideas from this angle, which the couple may then be able to pursue. The obvious examples are hymns, scripture readings and, if there are any, other readings.

The issue increasingly arises of an appropriate marriage rite when a divorced person is involved. Those churches which perform such marriages have their own proposals. For those which at present do not, there is a service of blessing. This is a theological nonsense, but it may for the time being be pastorally necessary and effective. Three points may be noted. First, whatever the minister's views on marriage and divorce, the fact is that divorces do occur and that the church—at least, the Church of England—is in confusion about its views. The minister, therefore, has to be sensitive lest his own and the church's confusion is projected into vulnerable people. Secondly, there is a more technical matter. With the ease of world-wide travel and different approaches to divorce in various countries, it is becoming increasingly complicated to disentangle the legal questions as to who is eligible to be married under British law. Any minister, therefore, intending to conduct a wedding, as opposed to a blessing, for a divorced person should be wary and check the details with the Registrar. And thirdly, whatever the rights or wrongs, there seems nothing in principle different in the process of ministering with a couple, one or both of whom has been divorced, than with those approaching matrimony for the first time.

Feed-back

Of the occasional offices a wedding is the one where those concerned are most likely to move away. Problems of housing and employment often make this inevitable. A consequence is that the couple have to develop their new relationship in some isolation from familiar surroundings and friends. This may be a contributory factor to the intensely personal understanding of marriage that prevails and which make marriages potentially fragile as institutions.

To leave the matter there, however, would be to fall into the trap of thinking that the one-to-one connection is the only important aspect of a brief encounter. How the minister acts in these offices is more widely known than he may suspect and it influences other facets of his ministry. He may receive direct feed-back from the friends and relations of the couple. More importantly, because he is known to be concerned with marrying, he may also be expected from time to time to comment on marriage and counsel married people. This is not a book on such counselling, and the point may merely be noted. If, however, adequate attention is given by the minister to his public role in the performance of the rite, then the future of marriages as human institutions will also be affected. Too easily the counselling response attracts ministers. Jack Dominian notes the danger of this seduction, when he calls his chapter on marriage preparation 'Preventing Breakdown'.[21] The concern which clergy demonstrate for acquiring skills in counselling marital breakdown may itself be evidence for a loss of confidence in the more mundane role of minister, as this has been described. But the question needs to be asked as to the extent to which abdication from their role in the occasional office may indicate that ministers are inadvertently contributing to marital breakdown. There is not much point in learning how to quench fires that one is lighting oneself.

Most weddings are celebrations. Even if they are not, the powerful investment in the couple may allow all concerned, including the minister, to overlook issues that are aroused. High on the list are questions of authority and guilt. Marriage in western society brings together in a unique way both private and social issues. It is, therefore, difficult for people to sort these out in themselves and in their relationships. The emphasis in this discussion on pastoral work has been on affirming the couple's authority, their individual responsibility for their decision to marry, and their joint responsibility as ministers of the sacrament. Problems of authority and its exercise are endemic in contemporary society. If, however, people are believed to be created in the image of God, as the Judaeo-Christian tradition consistently avows, then the nature of this assigned authority is a vital concern. This is especially so if the concept of 'the image of God' is linked to the primal pair of male and female. To be made in this image is to be given authority to be human. Yet that authority is constantly diminished or perverted. This comprises the essence of the doctrine of sin. As people approach marriage, a pervading sense is one of disarray, anxiety, sometimes unworthiness and even guilt. It may be argued that the church itself induces that guilt, but, whatever the church's contribution, it seems more likely that some such guilt is felt as human beings approach the creation of a new human institution for which they have to take public responsibility. In other words, weddings raise the issue of debased and refused authority in human beings, and one of the ministries sought from the church is forgiveness for failure and absolution. This is no simple matter of confession and ritual absolution. But we may understand such forgiveness as the reaffirmation on God's part that the authority which he assigns to all his creatures really is theirs. They are given it and invited confidently to act upon it.

It may be, therefore, that the church, when it encounters individuals and couples for a wedding, may be ministering to more profound matters, which belong to all men and women. The feed-back from this occasional office consequently may be more than a response from the couple or their relations and friends. It may become a constituent for the grasp of ministry as a whole, with which the church and its ministers operate in a locality. If so, weddings become far more than a chore. They are instances for the acting out of God's trust in his creatures and the discovery of that authority which he has assigned to his creatures, both individually and socially. Properly perceived, therefore, weddings offer opportunities for all involved to explore what it means to be human in the light of God's revelation. They are, therefore, of the essence of Christian ministry.

Notes

1. In addition to the two major reports from the Church of England (see above ch. 4, n. 2), note also Pope John Paul II, *Familiaris Consortio* (London, Catholic Truth Society, 1981); *Change in Marriage* (National Marriage Guidance Council, 1982). On marital problems and their contexts see J. Dominian, *Marital Breakdown* (Harmondsworth, Pelican, 1968); id., *Marital Pathology* (London, DLT, 1980); id., *Make or Break* (London, SPCK, 1984).
2. W. K. Lowther Clarke, 'Solemnisation of Matrimony', in W. K. Lowther Clarke, ed., *Liturgy and Worship* (London, SPCK, 1932), pp. 458ff.
3. Maureen Green, *Marriage* (London, Fontana, 1984), ch. 1.
4. On the impact of the pair in any context see W. R. Bion, *Experiences in Groups* (London, Tavistock, 1969), pp. 111ff. On the way in which the couple embodies a human search for profound levels of interpersonal relationship see A. D. and L. L. Colman, *Love and Ecstasy* (New York, Seabury, 1975).
5. Figures from Green, *Marriage.*
6. The national figures on how marriages are solemnized are published every five years as an appendix to the *Registrar General's Statistical Review of England and Wales.* The trend is towards more weddings in registry offices, with the Church of England performing most church weddings. The figures, however, are very confused by regional variation and the church's attitudes to the marriage of divorcees. See Barker, 'Proper Wedding', pp. 57ff and p. 223, nn. 11 and 12; also *Marriage and the Church's Task,* pp. 12ff, especially the warning in para. 30.
7. Green, *Marriage,* p. 31.
8. R. A. K. Runcie, Archbishop of Canterbury, in *The General Synod Report of Proceedings* 14 (1983), pp. 447f.
9. S. Platten, 'The Church's response to current divorce trends', *Crucible* (1984), pp. 82ff.
10. *Marriage, Divorce and the Church,* p. 14.
11. The word 'fantasy' is used in a general sense to refer to a wish, always in the end informed by the unconscious, which is distorted by defensive processes.
12. G. Gorer, *Sex and Marriage in England Today* (London, Nelson, 1971). *Marriage and the Church's Task,* pp. 17ff.
13. Colin Morris, *God-in-a-Box* (London, Hodder & Stoughton, 1984), pp. 25f.
14. Useful advice may be found in Michael Hocking, *A Handbook of Parish Work* (London, Mowbray, 1974), pp. 99ff. Technical information for the clergyman is in *Halsbury's Ecclesiastical Law* (London, Butterworth, 1975), or from the local registrar.
15. The annual publication from the British Medical Association, *Getting Married,* contains useful information which is, however, embedded in certain assumptions about weddings in a consumer society.

16. Dominian, *Make or Break,* ch. 8.
17. The notion of a holding environment is widely employed in family therapy. It derives from Winnicott's work on the caretaking function of the parent. For an explanation and example see E. R. Shapiro, 'The holding environment and family therapy with acting out adolescents', *International Journal of Psychoanalytic Psychotherapy* 9 (1982), pp. 209ff.
18. Green, *Marriage,* pp. 83ff.
19. G. J. Cuming, *A History of Anglican Liturgy,* 2nd edn, (London, Macmillan, 1982), p. 220.
20. Perham, *Liturgy,* p. 97.
21. Dominian, *Make or Break,* ch. 19.

EIGHT

Funerals

When baptizing, the minister has to face a series of theological problems about the nature of the gospel and its relation to everyday human experience. Confronted by those who wish to marry, his difficulty may be seen in terms of authority: if they are the ministers of the sacrament, what exactly is his role? Funerals, at least in the contemporary urban setting, present him with a sense that his theology and his authority are both swamped by the power of the emotion of grief and its social accompaniments.

There is a host of books about death, grief and mourning. Training officers report increased eagerness on the part of clergy to attend courses on bereavement counselling. It is difficult to participate in any gathering of clergy at which stories of funerals and half-serious jokes about undertakers (not to mention funeral fees) are not told. But if churches exist through interaction with their environment, we should not be surprised to find such matters becoming increasingly prominent. It is a modern commonplace (although not an accurate one) that, whereas the Victorians were preoccupied with death, twentieth-century man has become obsessed with sex. But such is the rate of change in society that even attitudes towards death and bereavement seem to alter rapidly. Since ministry is always exercised in a social context, the church's ministry through funerals will itself be subject to similar change.

The 1960s and 1970s were a period of optimism in many ways. Sexuality may have become a more prominent issue. Sanction was certainly given for a variety of behaviours which were characterized as 'the permissive society'. But in that setting death and its associated rituals became an embarrassment for many. It was not a taboo subject, but nor was it one which attracted interest. At one level certain customs disappeared—the wearing of black as a matter of respect, armbands, and raising the hat as a hearse passed. On a different plane the imminence of death as a result of nuclear war was ignored, except by campaigners, whose number decreased. In that environment some professional people, however,—psychoanalysts, psychologists, doctors and journalists—were constrained to stress the importance of being able to face death, the place of ritual, and the care needed by the bereaved.[1] Twenty years later those books have come into their own. Death is an issue that makes headlines. Medical developments, which are publicized, have made people unsure of what constitutes death and even when it occurs. The commonsense ideas about death have been displaced by a sense that personal mortality is in the hands of technicians. Megadeaths, a new coinage, are now a factor in people's thinking, which leads to a corresponding fatalism. It is no longer shocking when a character in a play hopes to be 'pissed and right underneath the first bomb'.[2] In every way death is a prominent issue in contemporary society. As a result, the particular deaths which occur and which generate the grief with which the minister is confronted, may carry other anxieties and anguishes.

Life's final transition is into the unknown. All other transitions to some degree reflect this ultimate process of separation. Death provides the basic model. But equally these other, intermediate separations inform the way that that model is construed. So, for example, the world is acutely aware of the possibility of its total destruction. Change in society seems to devalue what has been achieved in the past, and the personnel which are available for further work appear to be unwanted. These transitions may, therefore, reasonably be expected to be reinforced by the fact of death and at the same time people might also become unsure about death itself, how to face it and what bereavement means. The uncertainty of death itself is compounded by these additional factors, which contribute to a heightened level of anxiety.[3] Interest in spiritualism and the respectability now accorded to studies of existence after death do little to alter the basic issue for the minister.[4] This is that people look to a symbolic figure to have assurance and claim knowledge, which in the nature of the case no human being can possess.

In conducting funerals the minister is caught up in a greater range of issues than might immediately be apparent. Some of these are within him, as a human being who has to face his own death. But he will probably have only the most fleeting and almost professionally ritualistic contact with the bereaved, and probably none at all with the dying. When he is allowed to minister to a dying person, he today counts it a rare privilege. It is, therefore, with the inevitably brief encounter of the funeral service that we are concerned. The grief of the family is the point of contact. But they, even in the distress of their bereavement, are not divorced from the world, however much they may feel it and behave as if they were.

This chapter is not intended to supplement the already large literature on bereavement counselling and the pastoral care of the dying and the bereaved. This is discussed only as it affects the occasional office of the funeral. Since the minister is more exposed here than is sometimes apparent from the idealized context of dying, which is often implicit in books on the subject, it is especially vital for him to be sure of what he is handling. Most funerals in the country are still conducted by a religious figure, usually a Christian. In some places clergy have found themselves asked to conduct the funeral of a person from another faith, which can acknowledge him as a holy man. They are certainly accustomed to ministering to those of no obvious belief. The minister seems to represent something significant, albeit something of which most remain at a conscious level ignorant. Stories abound which demonstrate that his is a complex role, which is largely delineated by others. He is, for example, believed to be able to manage this final boundary to life. This may be a residual belief from the days when he would have been called to assist the dying to depart from this world. Clergy are still surprised to find that elderly people may regard a house communion as an implied viaticum and accordingly refuse the offer. But the minister is seen as more than a manager of such things. He is also looked to as a man of professed faith, who is believed to be able to face the spectre of death and, as it were, to defeat it. Whereas ordinary people are afraid of death and dying, the minister is supposed not to be. He is expected to be competent, even though he knows in himself that he is as human as anyone else. His believed strength in the face of death and his ability to be able to handle it produce a curious amalgam in people's minds, whereby he may almost become the purveyor of death, the death-man. As such he is both needed and shunned. These, and similar fantasies, make the minister a potent symbol in the context of death. By contrast, his own struggle with his faith and his humanity consistently remind him of his weakness and vulnerability. The pressure upon him, therefore, is to respond by acting a part, so that he may meet the expectations of his audience and not be hurt himself. There is probably no future in such a stance for any human being, and certainly for Christian ministry it has no profit.

The minister, when summoned for a funeral, joins a process that is already in progress and does so at a specific point. Studies of bereavement have shown how lengthy the total process is, even though in our society ritualized mourning is brief. The clergyman may be assigned about half an hour for the ritual and possibly a little more for an associated visit. But mourning lasts between two and five years, and the first two weeks, during which the minister's involvement occurs, is the time of greatest shock, denial and numbness.[5] In order to find his bearings in this context, the minister may use a generalized theory of the bereavement process. One danger, however, is that he may inadvertently become glib about death. Being able, as he believes, to locate a bereaved person within a theoretical construction, may suggest that he has accurately diagnosed their condition. The minister may then isolate himself by applying the appropriate 'treatment'. This is a caricature of ministry, but one which is occasionally met. It is almost as if the old defensive professionalism of the priest, who reads a standard service, has given place to a new form of so-called 'caring professionalism', by which the 'patient' is identified, diagnosed and treated. Understanding of the process, which may help provide the minister with an internal frame of reference, is useful only as a means of assisting him locate himself in relation to each particular, individual and unique bereavement.

Although within the long and varied process of bereavement

the funeral occupies only a little time, its significance is disproportionate to its length. Whatever the theoretical ideal, the funeral in practice takes place early in the period of mourning. It, therefore, functions to crystallize the immediate realities, such as the fact that someone actually has died and that the living have to do something about it. At the same time, in the confused dislocations of death, it provides a fixed reference point to which people can and do refer, as they work out their sense of bereavement. It becomes part of the folklore of the family, or, to use another metaphor, one of the sets of spectacles through which the dead person is remembered. What shape, therefore, those spectacles take is important for the lives of those reintegrating themselves into everyday life.[6]

This simple observation reinforces an obvious but important point about this rite: the funeral is for the bereaved and not for the corpse. The minister is not dismissing a soul from this world, nor is he merely disposing of mortal remains. He is not dealing with 'death' as some abstract phenomenon. He is in touch with a human experience of profound significance, which all, including he himself, have to undergo—the experience of loss and bereavement. The funeral, therefore, is for those who are left. Their emotions are being handled, and that perspective will naturally colour what is done in each instance.

The Approach

The funeral is quite unlike the other two offices in the approach phase. There are no parents seeking something for their child, or a couple looking for an opportunity for themselves. The usual approach to a minister comes as the result of something that has already occurred and is complete in itself: the person has died; the family are coping; the undertaker has the details in hand; and then the minister is contacted, usually by the undertaker. This contact with the bereaved is mediated. That fact may affect the relationship that may be established between the minister and the bereaved. For he may appear to be an imposed necessity and may feel himself to be such. He is there because a funeral has to be performed. Often he is not known or in any personal sense wanted.

Any encounter between the minister and the bereaved has to be negotiated in a context which encourages both parties to assume that the negotiation has already taken place. This creates obvious tensions. Relationships need time for their construction, and there is usually no time, especially in a busy parish. The bereaved themselves are in a distressed state and probably do not feel like making a new relationship with a stranger, albeit a needed one. And inevitably expectations of the encounter will be coloured by half-remembered experiences from previous times of grief and, more immediately, from impressions given by the undertaker. For most people the experience of bereavement is one of chaos. One effect of people's being generally unfamiliar with death and how to deal with it, even at a formal level, is that they tend to surrender their responsibilities to others, who take them over effectively, swiftly and competently. But in so doing they deprive people of their own authority and responsibility as relatives of one who has died. At the same time such efficiency may enable the bereaved to feel fine, since any other burdens in addition to grief seem unnecessarily harsh. But in the long run this relief can have a deleterious effect, as people develop an irrational sense of guilt that they should have done more, been more deeply involved, or looked after the deceased better. The minister, as a so-called 'expert', may have a constructive role in this phase. He is brought in because he knows about funerals, and that is the base for his offer of ministry. But many of the arrangements for that funeral will not be in his hands. He may take this as a personal slight and fight for a position of more acknowledged competence among the group of those who are handling the bereavement. On the other hand, he may acknowledge his freedom to represent ultimate human issues of responsibility in a chaotic context of experience, and thus use the occasion for effective (which is not the same as efficient) ministry.

The task of this approach phase within the sequence of the funeral arrangements may be described as that of enabling the bereaved to become conscious of their grief process in which they are caught up. This is their responsibility as human beings and in their roles as relatives or friends of the deceased. To facilitate this, however, there are a number of points to which the minister may attend.

Early in the bereavement those responsible for making the funeral arrangements have much to consider. Most funeral directors are careful in guiding them through the legal and other requirements that follow a death. There are many of these, and people often comment on the sense of rush that results. The days seem like a race to get things done in time for the funeral; the nights are long and, especially for a widow or widower, lonely. The British are said to be poor at facing the need to grieve and express feelings. In this maelstrom of activity the bereaved need space in which to grieve and on occasions permission to do so.[7] The prevailing culture tends to diminish death. The euphemisms and the reassurances that it is somehow unreal are familiar. One consequence is that grieving may be omitted at the early stage of loss. The minister, as the 'death man', is often the one who can give permission to grieve. The funeral, for which he is needed, is an occasion for public grieving, whatever else it may be. It is the final leave-taking from all that was tangible of a human being, whose life affected others. To facilitate this process the minister needs to listen when he meets the relatives of the deceased, and especially members of the wider family. If he can begin to discern tensions and conflicts, as well as expressions of hope and unsuspected affection, he may be able to construct in his own mind a rough grid of relationships and so place the deceased within it. This will assist him to imbue the formality of grieving in the course of the funeral with necessary reality.

During this phase the minister is also expected to manage certain things. The pressure upon him is to collude with disowning behaviour on the part of the bereaved, which shows itself in a desire to leave the details of the funeral to the minister. However understandable such attitudes may seem in the emotion of the moment, and however much the caring dimension of the minister may instinctively respond to it, this has to be resisted. Ritual, especially that surrounding death, is not merely a containing framework for human grief, to which it is applied with more or less skill by the minister. It is created by those concerned—the bereaved and the more detached symbolic figure of the minister—as a means of enabling a major transition to be accomplished. The experience of the bereaved at an early stage is that of shock and denial. Their lives feel deformed and shapeless. In that setting the funeral liturgy may provide a framework which, however little it is consciously appreciated, may nevertheless assure people that there is some shape to human existence which can be recovered. But if the ritual is to perform this function, then the bereaved have also to begin to make it their own. A small illustration is that of the role of chief mourner, who often comes into his own at the reception after the funeral. The minister is often invited to this, but when there is ignored. It is as if the host or hostess, as chief mourner, somehow takes over from the minister the role of providing shape to life by emphasizing the familiar and customary. If, then, the bereaved are to make the earlier ritual of the funeral their own, too, they not only need information about the options available but also to sense the partnership with the minister, so that they can authorize him to act on their behalf as well as for the larger unknowns of society, humanity and God. His theological and spiritual resource for sustaining such a role may thus be made available to the bereaved.

Exploring the Meaning

Since the encounter with people during this occasional office is so brief, it is not possible (except for the sake of discussion) to separate this second phase from the approach. The minister may on rare occasions have already established a relationship which allows the meaning of bereavement and death to be explored before, during and after the funeral. But for most this is a luxury. In the customary very brief encounter the chances are that only one pre-funeral visit is possible. Since people are not likely to be able to take in very much at such a time, it follows that one of the chief tasks in this phase is to allow them to express as much as they wish or are able. In order to give permission to grieve, the minister holds certain realities on behalf of the bereaved. This is more difficult than it sounds, since there often appears to be an expectation that he will confirm their fantasies. As a human being he, too, will be to some degree uncertain about questions of death and its meaning. And even if he holds that his gospel provides him with certainties, he will not be able, for reasons which will become apparent, to present an apologia for them in the hope of sharing them at this stage with bereaved people.

The most difficult reality to face is that the dead person has died. For that reason the minister has to be unafraid of employing words like 'dead' or 'died'. This is particularly important for the funeral of a Christian believer, since much contemporary Christianity seems to think of death as a temporary break in life, and in so doing conforms to popular superstition rather than to the gospel. The minister has in the doctrine of the resurrection of the body an acknowledgement of death's reality. Tom Baker has expressed this succinctly:

> The doctrine of the resurrection of the body (of the whole person, if you like) authenticates our sense of poignant loss, because it is concerned precisely with the transformation of what has been lost. Nostalgia is often trivial and self-indulgent. But it is a very human emotion, and points to something real, of which we need not feel ashamed.[8]

The minister may have his own understanding of an approach to life and death, crucifixion and resurrection. But for the ministry which he is offering to the bereaved, this is a resource for assisting them to face the reality of death and not a means of colluding in avoiding it.

A second facet of the exploration is enabling people to realize that the process on which they have embarked is a long one. Immediate understanding, therefore, is not merely unlikely: it is actually impossible. Permission to grieve thus becomes something more than allowing people to cry. It is also encouraging them to recognize that, as a result of the deceased having died, there is a permanent, long-term felt loss, which the bereaved may try to fill in a number of ways. These may be in trying to deal with the residue of the relationship through other (usually unsuitable) people or in seeing visions. The content of this period of mourning is often very general. Bereaved people are not usually able to focus on specifics. But this is itself one means of allowing themselves space in the busy-ness of preparation for the funeral, so that through reflection they may provide for themselves points to which to refer back as they journey through the bereavement process.

One pressure on the minister at this point is to make statements that he cannot justify or promises that he cannot keep. Asked 'Will I see my loved one again, when I die?', he is inclined to soothe by answering affirmatively. But pastoral sensitivity and theological perception both demand a gentle 'No'. Some parts of the deceased person have gone for ever: the body is decaying, and as a result the relationship of embodied people is ended.[9] Belief in the resurrection of the body is no reason to deny, or imply that it is desirable to deny, the actual sense of ending, loss and permanence of death. The minister may also wish to assure the bereaved of divine care by promising what he cannot fulfil. One customary guarantee is that he will make a post-funeral visit. Sometimes such a call can be valuable, and this is discussed later. But for most clergy these visits are a sheer impossibility. To promise one, therefore, or even appear to, is probably the minister's self-protection. Rather than an instance of genuine pastoral activity, such a suggestion merely creates further unreality in the situation.

The key to the exploration phase of a funeral is the way in which the minister manages himself in role. The emotional impact of the encounter is greater than in the case of the other offices. Because of the way that society handles death, the temptation before the minister is to defend against any intrusion into his own self by adopting an apparently professional role. In this ministry, however, the pastor brings his own human and spiritual vulnerability to bear with people at their most fragile.[10] The separation of death may be compared with a stripping off of part of oneself or even of separation from the self. In such a ministry, the minister is exposed to his own humanity. 'Every man's *death* diminishes *me*', and the minister who is regularly involved with death is bound to experience that diminishing.[11] To compensate he may seek counselling skills, although they are not really required. Alternatively he may look to invulnerable (as he believes) theological positions, which are immune from scrutiny or scepticism. The outcome, however, is a brittle person, whose reliability may be felt to be suspect on the part of those who seek some ministry.

One area in which such disturbance manifests itself is in believed competition with funeral directors. Relationships between undertakers and ministers are inevitably close, if not intimate. The minister may be so confined in his own self-perception that he may overlook the obvious fact that funeral directors are usually the first ministers in any bereavement, just as the police may take this role at a sudden or accidental death. To ignore or discount such ministries because they appear theologically unauthenticated limits the pastor's own ministering. Since, however, it is difficult to express to the bereaved, or with them, the strong feelings which a death generates in the pastor, there is a risk that these may be directed at the undertaker or back at oneself. In the former case, this can produce futile contretemps, which may make the clergy feel better but which will not further overall ministry in an area. In the latter instance, this introverted anger may produce apathy, which then diverts energy from a vital piece of public ministry. In either case, a minister in the exploration phase of the encounter over a funeral might usefully ask himself what he is doing with his own powerful, human emotions.

The approach phase is essentially one of collaboration with the bereaved and with others, such as the undertaker. The minister may experience ambivalent feelings directed at him. On the one hand he may be treated almost as the only one who understands at any depth and can deal effectively with the death. If he colludes with that, he may not only diminish the bereaved people's responsibility and so not help them. He may also cease to work with others and find himself antipathetic to them. On the other hand, he may feel brought in as a necessary, but unfortunate factor, in the production of a funeral, which is mostly out of his hands and control. Some resentment at such an attitude is not unnatural, but it may become compounded by a sense of insult to his gospel of resurrection. To survive this felt onslaught, he may try and escape the human emotions which are his and so avoid encountering those of others. Either way, the minister may feel especially ineffective at this point in the bereavement process. If, however, he can grasp that such feelings are part of the complex and chaotic experience of bereavement, he may be able to discover through them what is happening. For he will be able to give direct attention to the practical question, which is a sure guide in all Christian ministry: 'What is happening to me, and why?' Self-interpretation in role is the clue to ministry in exploring the meaning of death and bereavement.[12]

The Rite

In thinking of funerals it is especially useful to distinguish between 'rite' and 'ritual'. The ritual is the funeral itself, with all its accompaniments — undertakers, flowers, minister, service in church or chapel, and wake or funeral tea. The rite, however, is a wider concept, covering the extended process of transition from the initial separation to reincorporation into society. The ritual plays a fundamental part in the rite. Because contemporary western society remains unsure about how to think of death and how people should behave in the face of it, a range of rituals has been created. Two, for example, concern the disposal of the corpse (burial or cremation) and the place where the ritual is held (church, crematorium or home). Although each of these options seems simple, they shroud a range of unexplored questions. Burial or cremation, for example, both dispose of the corpse but each conveys diverse images of value and exemplify different archetypes.

A funeral is a social occasion. Local customs vary, but associations extend beyond the family. Colleagues from work, miscellaneous social contacts, other friends and acquaintances, people from the street, are all likely to attend a funeral. Announcements of death still form a major component of the personal columns in local newspapers. The funeral, which hitherto the minister might have conceived in terms of the family and the deceased, affects more people. As the family think with the minister about the ritual, this perspective may be lost. The pastor, therefore, may have deliberately to introduce it or at least hold onto it. For example, there is little point in an intimate family group wishing to sing a favourite, but obscure, hymn which the dead person enjoyed, when the minister knows that few, if any, of those attending from other backgrounds will know or understand it. There are other ways of incorporating such requests, as, for example, in a reading or as part of any music played. The family and more casual acquaintances will thus both be able to participate.

This minor example indicates the role of the minister in the funeral service. He directs it. There may be close collaboration in the design of the ritual, but its performance lies in the minister's hands. For the bereaved there are many discomforting aspects to a funeral, which range from feelings aroused by the final acknowledgement that the body has gone to anxieties about proper behaviour in public. Through the ritual the minister is asked to articulate on behalf of people what they cannot at this moment manage for themselves. The funeral, therefore, is a singular instance of managed worship.

Reflections on worship as an instance of managed regression illuminate the minister's task. The term 'regression' sounds pejorative and is only used with hesitation. But it best describes the process of such worship, which has been delineated by Bruce Reed.[13] Human development consists in progression from childhood and dependence upon parents to adult acknowledgement of interdependence between responsible people, and not, as some might think, to independence from others. As mature adults human beings live in an oscillation between these two states of dependence and autonomy. Regression to dependence, therefore, is not a reversion to infantile behaviour, but an aspect of adult life, which requires affirmation and recognition. Worship and ritual have their place in this scheme. They provide specific occasions of and opportunity for controlled regression. Through ritual people may experience the surrender of sophisticated interpretation, or the facade that they are capable of this, and allow thoughts and feelings to range in a managed context of images and ideas. Considered in this light, a funeral service is not an event but a means by which a process may be undergone. In order to facilitate this regression and the move back towards recovery of responsibility and autonomy, a containing environment is created. Liturgy performs this function, both through the way in which it is conducted and with its unfamiliar richness of ideas and images. Impressions and conveyed ideas, especially at a funeral, are more important than meanings.

Bereaved people are human beings in a disoriented state. The minister is invited to stand for them on a boundary where they feel at present unable to stand and to manage a process on their behalf. Although such feelings are acute in the immediate family, the congregation will also include people at different stages of grief and with various degrees of involvement with the deceased. The minister cannot prescribe what should be experienced, but he creates a context in which people may integrate themselves in any needful fashion. To achieve this the minister presents the reality of death as a fact of human existence. He cannot employ distracting euphemisms. He also has to articulate feelings on behalf of the bereaved, and among these will certainly be a sense of uncertainty, confusion and disarray. At the same time, his job is to do this without letting it degenerate merely into an emotional outburst on their behalf. The awe of present reality does not obliterate the future, when for the bereaved life continues. The pastor's ability to do this depends upon the way the approach phase has been handled. But people, especially under stress, also surrender to him an alarming amount of power, which he has to hold with astuteness. As a Christian he may be tempted to respond with almost glib talk of life after death, rather than a profound exploration of the gospel emphasis that life is in the midst of death. He has, therefore, to be particularly sensitive in this ministry to the feelings of others and at the same time bold in taking risks of judgement. He has to prove reliable and dependable, but only in such a way that people may, through the ritual, begin to resume their own responsibilities.

How this is achieved in each instance will depend upon the people with whom he is dealing and local conditions. One or two general points, however, may be listed. Inevitably a funeral will be affected by local customs. In preparing the service, therefore, the minister may have to negotiate them into the liturgy. It is, however, crucial that people, if they are to be able to use the process as an occasion for handling grief and preparing for the future, participate. Under the immediate stress of grief they sometimes ask the minister merely to do what is proper and to keep it short and simple. There is much to be said for both brevity and simplicity, not least in liturgy. But behind the request may lie an attempt to escape grieving, to which the pastor will give attention. Even within the limitations of an urban cremation service the minister has time available, the use of which can be planned. The congregation should participate in the service itself. To say together the Lord's Prayer or a short psalm may be the minimum. But people should not at this juncture be required to attempt even familiar words from memory, and for many there will probably be no such familiar texts. Few, if any, today know the Lord's Prayer by heart and none will probably be able to manage it in an agreed version. A text, therefore, is essential, and the congregation may need directing to it. Such guidance should also extend to posture. If the service is to be an occasion of such managed regression as has been described, it should not feel disrupted by too much movement. Clear directions on standing and sitting (kneeling is not often advisable) will assist people to experience the dislocation of parting without being diverted towards additional anxieties about how they should be behaving. The minister is managing the process, but not the people, in so acting.

Society's disarray with death emerges in the debate about the place where a funeral should be held. Some evidence is beginning to appear that people are increasingly dissatisfied with a service at a crematorium, but are unclear about what they wish to replace it. It may be, especially with the amount of travelling involved, that funerals should be encouraged in the deceased's locality—that is, the local church—and followed by committal at the crematorium or graveyard. It has been proposed by some that cremation should precede the funeral, but there seems little enthusiasm for this and the image of a funeral service around an urn, rather than the corpse, seems strange. It is, however, important that, whatever arrangements are made, the bereaved family should, as a general rule, watch the disposal of the body through burial or its reception to the crematorium. Any ritual, which does not include this formal separation from mortal remains, is deficient.

For all mourners the service should allow three expressions of feeling and time for reflection on them. First there is the sense of thanksgiving. This must vary according to the circumstances of death, but there are few human beings who cannot be recalled without some thankfulness. In the resolution phase of bereavement people need to come to terms with their anger and resentments and with the fact that business with the deceased remains unsatisfactorily incomplete. Expression of thanksgiving is not the same as idealizing the deceased. His limitations and faults can be named, but equally they can be incorporated into critical thanksgiving. For they were major components of who he was. The funeral, however, may deliberately focus upon thanksgiving in this sense, as a means of encouraging at a later stage the facing of these and similar guilts. Secondly, time is needed to recall what the dead person was to those who are bereaved. This implies sorrow and joy, as well as a sense of fulfilment and loss. Such emotions can be expressed, if space is deliberately made for them in the funeral service. For this offers momentarily secure room for the legitimate examination of such feelings. Thirdly, there is the fact that everyone has to confront his or her own death. This particular dying, therefore, is to be set in the context of all human mortality. Which of the available liturgies best furthers these tasks is not a matter for theoretical dispute. The choice is one of pastoral judgement. It may be, as some report, that different liturgies are suitable for different occasions, and that their variety is a positive asset.

One specific question which concerns some ministers is whether (and if so, how) they are to preach at a funeral service. The order in the Book of Common Prayer has no place for a sermon, but the modern rites make it an option. Each minister is himself responsible for the way in which he believes that the proclamation of the gospel is best served, and will make his own decision. Four general observations, however, may be offered.

First, how the gospel is verbalized and conceptualized is a

matter of dispute, but Christians agree that it does not consist of words alone. At the centre of the Christian message is the Word, which could only be encountered when it became enfleshed. Words are by that incarnation acknowledged, but not overvalued. The primary proclamation of the gospel in a funeral, whatever the minister may or may not articulate, will be the confidence that he embodies in the face of death. Because of the emotional dislocation experienced by the bereaved, they can rarely hear what is actually said. Odd remarks may stick, but it appears that people remember demeanour and attitude more than content. The reason for this is that at the time of the funeral bereaved people are struggling to create a structure for their survival. For that they will use whatever reinforces resources that are already within them. To ask them at this moment to adopt an unfamiliar structure is to invite its rejection. If, then, the minister feels in himself the general human sense of mortality, which any death generates, and embodies in himself the hope that his gospel holds out within that mortality, then he will chiefly convey this through the way he manages the process and the manner in which he conducts the ritual.

Secondly, the gospel itself is more vulnerable in the area of death than its ministers sometimes recognize. The Christian message has a tendency to gloss over death in its haste to reach the so-called joys of the resurrection.[14] Any minister needs to guard against this theological weakness in his message. Early use, for example, of the traditional opening sentence of the liturgy—'I am the resurrection and the life' (John 11.25f)—raises the question. On the one hand its familiarity may be part of the reassurance of the funeral for the bereaved. On the other hand, its early affirmation of resurrection and life may detract from the opportunities to face the actual death of the deceased. There is in the additional words suggested by the Alternative Service Book a preferable logical progression: the reality of death; the everlasting love of God; God's grace made known in Christ; and the Christian hope for all mankind.[15] In the face of uncertainty about death, the liturgy requires some clear statement that death is not a failure, but a natural outcome to every human life, none of which can lie beyond God's mercy.

A further dangerous area theologically forms the third point. Simple identification of Christ's believed experience with that of every person is a seduction. It is easily said, but is certainly not believable at the time of bereavement, that Jesus has undergone the same trauma as the bereaved. There is no evidence, other than as may be hinted by the extended story of Lazarus (John 11), that Jesus might have been bereaved. And bereavement is the focal issue in a funeral, rather than death. If the minister, in his preoccupation to present a relevant Christ, attempts it in this way, he will succeed in the very fault which he is trying to avoid. For he will depersonalize the ritual and make it less immediate for the bereaved, by appearing to suggest that their specific grief is merely an instance of some supposed greater grief, which was experienced on their behalf by Jesus Christ.

Finally, and most obviously, since it is not likely that those attending a funeral will be able to take in very much, the address, if there is to be one, has to be felt to be an intrinsic component of the liturgy and not an imposed extra. It will, therefore, be brief, carefully prepared, specific in its mention of the deceased and his or her family, and consciously structured into the particular funeral that is being conducted. If it is impossible to give such an address, as is often the case with duty funerals in a city crematorium, then it may be wiser to omit it and take greater care with the content of the service, the way people are guided through the ritual, and the prayers which are offered.

Feed-Back

Since the process of grieving is lengthy, some sort of post-funeral contact with the bereaved might seem particularly valuable as part of ministering to them. Many clergy reckon that this might be a better use of their time than the pre-funeral call, although they have no evidence for such a view. But they come up against the fact that time is limited. In the light of this the minister needs to recall the context within which he is working. It is not a one-to-one relationship with the bereaved. He has been used for what he represents of larger issues and horizons, as well as for the specific role in the ritual. He is, therefore, at the early stage involved with colleagues, such as the undertaker. Later these colleagues become the bereaved members of the family and their familiar contacts. If death is regarded as an inevitable component of life, then the feed-back phase of the process will be diffuse. When people are enabled to resume responsibility for their own existence, many of them do it effectively. Bereavement is not an illness, although it may sometimes turn morbid and require counselling or medication. But for most people it proves, despite first appearances, an assimilable and ultimately profitable experience.

In the post-funeral phase the minister, if the bereaved remain resident in the parish, might keep an eye open for them. It is noticeable, as has already been mentioned, that if the minister works effectively at the occasional offices, he tends to meet those with whom he has been involved in a variety of settings. But the main clues to any further explicit work will be picked up in the approach phase and the ritual itself. For example, if the bereaved person seems to be alone—perhaps a widow without relatives—then it may be that the minister might make a brief call on the evening of the funeral. But if, however, friends and neighbours attend the funeral, then it is a reasonable assumption that ministry after the funeral will be carried out through neighbours exercising the natural care that small communities provide. This, however, may itself need to be assessed with care by the vicar. Figures from one survey, for example, suggest that about 37% of people found themselves without help or advice when they were bereaved.[16] If this is a local phenomenon, a church might consider a scheme of lay visitors to provide support for any who appear to need it. But even such an apparently simple and caring idea needs careful forethought. For an increasingly important characteristic within the welfare society is the development of voluntary societies for and associations of those suffering particular stress, deprivation or need. Cruse, for example, has been established for widows and their children. A number of bodies are specially concerned with infant and child death, and for the elderly such societies as Age Concern exist. These national organizations, with their local groups, are often supplemented by a neighbourhood initiative. The minister should at least be aware of what is provided.[17] In such a way he may be able to further existing, though not necessarily church-based, ministry rather than find himself, for the best of motives, in competition.

Of the occasional offices funerals can appear the least rewarding for the Christian minister. The extreme vulnerability of the bereaved makes him wary of exploiting, or seeming to exploit, them. His own personal involvement, because death is common to him (as to all), is expressed in a liturgical framework, which may seem unsatisfactory. Grim services in dingy chapels do not encourage a sense that he is about anything to do with ultimate meaning, whether in this world or the next. The amalgam of superstition associated with the hereafter, coupled with the problems of Christian belief about life after death, compound his personal questioning. Yet at the same time he feels used as a pillar of reliability and assurance in a dark moment of life. If, however, he can avoid merely colluding with expectations, either because of his own uncertainties or because of an inability to resist the seductions of people's apparent, but probably not real, needs, the minister can find in this work genuine occasion for Christian ministry. For he is being invited to stand for people where, for the moment, they feel inadequate themselves and to interpret the common human experience, death and bereavement, in the light of his supposed ability to represent God and face the unknown. Such a stance is that both of the Christian minister and, when considered carefully, of Christ himself.

Notes

1. J. Mitford, *The American Way of Death* (London, Hutchinson, 1963); G. Gorer, *Death, Grief and Mourning in Contemporary Britain* (London, Cresset, 1965), H. Feifel, ed., *The Meaning of Death* (New York, McGraw-Hill, 1960); A. Toynbee et al., *Man's Concern with Death* (London, Hodder & Stoughton, 1968); E. Kubler-Ross, *On Death and Dying* (London, Tavistock, 1970).
2. A youth in B. Hines, *Threads* (BBCtv, 23 September, 1984)

3. J. B. McCarthy, *Death Anxiety: The Loss of the Self* (New York, Gardner Press, 1980). Although they are often in practice compounded, 'fear of death' and 'fear of annihilation' might usefully be distinguished.

4. J. Hick, *Death and Eternal Life* (London, Collins, 1976); P. Badham, *Christian Beliefs about Life after Death* (London, SPCK, 1978); P. and L. Badham, *Immortality or Extinction?* (London, Macmillan, 1982).

5. I. Ainsworth-Smith and P. Speck, *Letting Go* (London, SPCK, 1982), p. 13.

6. B. A. Backer, N. Hannon and N. A. Russell, *Death and Dying: Individuals and Institutions* (New York, Wiley, 1982), especially ch. 8.

7. O. S. Margolis et al., ed., *Acute Grief* (New York, Columbia University Press, 1981), especially Part IV.

8. T. G. A. Baker, ' "... and the life everlasting"?', *Theology* 86 (1983), pp. 425ff.

9. Baker, op. cit., p. 432.

10. S. A. Ross, 'The clergyman also mourns', in Margolis et al., ed., *Acute Grief*, pp. 225ff.

11. John Donne, *Devotions*.

12. *TPT*, p. 33.

13. Reed, *Dynamics*, pp. 23ff.

14. Moltmann, *Crucified God*, pp. 32ff.

15. 1 Tim. 6.7; Job 1.21; Deut. 33.27; Lam. 3.22f; Matt. 5.4; John 3.16; Rom. 8.38f; 1 Cor. 2.9; 1 Thess. 4.14ff.

16. P. J. Hennessy, *Families, Funerals and Finances* (London, HMSO, 1980), cited by Ainsworth-Smith and Speck, *Letting Go*, p. 81.

17. See the list in Ainsworth-Smith and Speck, op. cit., pp. 137ff. For the story of one such organization, Cruse, see M. Torrie, *To Begin Again* (London, Dent, 1970).

PART THREE

Handling the Pressures from the Occasional Offices

NINE

The Minister: Pressures and Resources

The work of the occasional offices must absorb much of the public minister's energy. Although some aspects of this ministry may be delegated, the nature of unconscious dependency, with which the church lives and works, is such that, if this ministry is to be exercised, the recognized religious figure will be heavily involved. Many ministers experience this ministry as demanding. Whether in an urban parish or in an apparently more comprehensible rural setting, the clergyman finds himself caught in a series of pressures. Not all experience every one of these to the same degree. But when their ministry is considered, most ministers find all or most of these pressures to be part of their everyday experience.

Pressure from Time

The encounters through requests for the occasional offices, although brief in that they are fleeting within the total scheme of people's lives and the scale of a minister's work, nevertheless take time. Diaries have to be managed, and people are not usually as accommodating as might be hoped. The competing demands for the minister's time are many and various. Ordinands are warned of the trap of busy-ness, but almost without fail ministers fall into it.[1] A practical effect of such earnestness, demonstrated by a full (often paraded) diary, is that the minister becomes less available to those who wish to approach him, while at the same time deceiving himself that he is accessible. But there is another, and more serious, consequence. The sense of reliability in the minister, which provides the link for people's felt, but unexpressed, dependency, is missing. As a result parishioners feel disabled from inviting him to work with them. It is not an uncommon experience for those training the clergy today to find that they eagerly come to courses on counselling, but that they often end by asking how, now that they are 'trained', they can find those whom to counsel. They overlook the obvious fact that, if ministers were to do their work in the parish, they would most probably meet through the occasional offices more people than any professional counsellor and most likely would be of more use to them. The issue is not so much lack of competence in the clergy, to be remedied by training, as a blindness to their role, often induced by a false sense of the need to be busy.

Spiritual directors tend to emphasize the need for the minister to find space and quiet. Those who look to him for ministry also seek this. Monica Furlong has written that 'the clergyman's role is to decrease his activity', and that she looks for a minister who can live in a state that is 'neither laziness nor hyper-activity'.[2] Many, if not most, ministers would probably concur that such a state is desirable. But the burden of the occasional offices seems to militate against its achievement. The question, however, when faced with such demand, is how brief but intense encounters can most effectively be managed. Clergy in general find difficulty in disengaging from individuals, and this may be reinforced by any training that implies that 'intense' means 'long in time'. Somewhere in the background lurks a psychoanalytic model. Time, however, as was noted earlier, is not inflexible. It changes according to perspective. If the notion of a process to be managed is given priority in considering the occasional offices, it may be that the apparent pressure of time may be seen for what it is—a question of how ministry is understood and priorities assigned.

Pressure from the Church

The minister cannot be isolated from the assumptive world of the church, of which he is a member. Later we shall consider the pressures of the local church. Here the point at issue is that ecclesiastical culture of synods, reports, discussions and ideas within which the local church is set. A prevailing ideology is that, if the church is to be more effective in the world, it should more clearly identify itself and draw its boundaries of belief, practice and membership. Then it would be more sure of what it has to offer and more confident in presenting it. Attention is consequently directed to the church's internal life, its organization, beliefs, liturgy, and criteria for membership. No minister, being a member of a particular church which is caught up in such debates, can be immune from these pressures. But it may help him to recall that any appreciation of the way that an enterprise interacts with its environment (what the church usually describes as ministry and mission), carries another fundamental implication: 'Significant internal changes within a system cannot be sustained unless consistent changes occur in the relatedness of the system to its environment.'3 This understanding suggests that the current trends in the churches need reversing and that risks once more have to be taken by engaging with people on the basis of their requests, demands and superstitions. When Christians bravely speak of losing all for the sake of the gospel, they neglect the obvious point that part of this 'all' will be those aspects of the believed gospel that they feel most inclined to preserve.

The clergy are necessarily, therefore, involved in contemporary questions about how ministry is to be exercised and in major matters of church order and doctrine. If they allow all this to be imported into their day-to-day stance with those who turn to the church — and hence to them — for some aspect of a largely undefined ministry, they will probably be inclined to devalue the significance of those requests in order to protect themselves from the confusions of faith and practice that are being engendered within them. To cope with such pressures, therefore, the minister will need in himself an ordered perception of the church as he knows and experiences it and of the task that it is performing.4 The conclusions he reaches may be less palatable than some of the weightier (and possibly flightier) views of church leaders, theologians and ecumenists. But without some such interpretative framework, he will have difficulty in sustaining Christian ministry against pressure from the church.

Pressure from the Minister

Amid the many welcome developments in thinking about ministry today, there lurks a major hazard. Anxious for good reason about being trapped in a false and inappropriate professionalism, the church's minister may encourage in himself the belief that he has no professional skill.[5] This may be a gratifyingly deprecatory stance for the humble individual and an encouraging view for those lay people who seek an alternative interest in life by acquiring office as some sort of authorized 'minister'. But it is undermining to any ministry by the church, which may be requested by ordinary people, who themselves represent the image of God. When faced by intense and unencompassable feelings, such as those around the future of a couple, a child as the embodiment of a new age, or death as entry to the unknown, people seek focal figures to enable them to handle them. This ministry is more than one of personal encounter. It contributes to the general belief systems of a society, which are significant both for individuals and for social groupings. It is here that the unspecific phrase 'fabric of society' becomes appropriate.[6] As a religious figure, the minister professes to be one in whom questions of meaning and of God (they are not unconnected) may be explored. As such he is publicly recognizable as an access point to the church and hence to the gospel. The phrase 'going into the church' as a description of ordination is unfortunate. But it contains a practical and pastoral truth about the role of the minister in relation to the church's task.

Sometimes ministers revolt against a role that is assigned to them, because they confuse in their thinking two separable systems in church life. There is on the one hand its public ministry, of which they are part, which provides these access points for people with their dependencies. On the other hand there is the support system, by which all who witness to the Christian faith, wherever they may be, are encouraged and enabled to be the church. As a Christian, the minister is also part of this system. If, however, he attempts to make the support system into the access system, by trying to delegate the occasional offices to the laity, he is usually disappointed.

The stress upon himself, which he is trying to reduce, is increased. He will have overlooked the nature of human expectations and in so doing will be closing down access points for the parishioners and confusing the church members. All then begin to feel incompetent: the parishioners, because they feel that they are unable to clarify their request in such a way as to get a response; the congregation because they find themselves unable to understand what the parishioners are requesting. Another outcome is the diminishing of the role of the public minister. It is today argued that the role of the minister of religion has already been reduced. There may be truth in the argument that, since society is changing, his role also alters.[7] But it sometimes appears that the reduction in the role of the ordained minister owes as much, if not more, to the withdrawal of the church's ministers from this position of primary interface with the non-church people than to any greater willingness on their part to have less to do with him.

Pressure from Emotions

Every minister, however he understands the church, his role and the need for some sort of management, nevertheless comes up against the fact that ministry through the occasional offices offers limited emotional satisfaction. In spite of sudden and unexpected gratification, this ministry more often seems characterized by heavy demands upon the minister's personal resources, which go unrewarded. The congregation usually expects him to do this work. Sometimes the minister may feel that contact with parishioners around baptisms, weddings and funerals is less fraught and burdensome than dealing with yet another committee of the believing people of God. But he has in the end to reckon that the encounters are short-lived, and that there is rarely a sense of work well done or of the people being eager to see him after he has performed his function. Sometimes very strange attitudes emerge. For example, a clergyman may find that the relatives of someone whose funeral he has conducted will cross the street in order to avoid him. Various ideas have been discussed throughout this book about why such eccentric behaviour occurs. But however adequately explanations may be developed and courses offered to assist ministers in appreciating human behaviour, the experience remains personally mystifying and not a little wounding. There may be, therefore, a tendency to shrink from this type of work for unexamined emotional reasons.

Intellectually a minister may be able to ask himself why he should expect gratification. He may even be masochistically seeking to justify his feeling of hurt by means of theological or spiritual arguments. But in spite of all this, he may still, whether consciously or not, deliberately involve himself in areas of ministry which seem more warmly appreciated. In so doing he may find himself in a double bind. On the one hand, he may ask questions about the significance of Christian ministry (and ordination in particular), which he may answer in terms which release him from the public encounter with parishioners and direct him to members of the congregation or other groups in which he feels welcome. Yet the further he is involved in these worlds, the more insistent questioning of the model of Jesus' ministry with sinners, rather than with the righteous, returns to haunt him.

Pressure from Theology

Throughout this essay theological points and discussions have been introduced in passing. But as an argument about pastoral practice, the book has been designed to allow the reader to raise his or her own theological questions. Here, however, after a brief consideration of the pressure upon the minister from theological issues, a transition will be made to three lines of approach, which any ministry has to take into account when dealing with human beings, and which are sometimes overlooked in theological reflections on ministry. These passages inevitably more than most draw upon the background of the Church of England. But that may be no bad thing, since the experience of this church in handling the occasional offices is, given the religious complexion of Great Britain, among the most extreme.[8]

It is a characteristic of any church, but not least one which contains so diverse a range of self-understandings, that theology is invoked by all parties as a believed external object, which may defend against work at the task in hand. In recent decades a distinctive, and to some disquieting, development has occurred. The long-standing dispute between the two main parties in the Church of England — the Evangelicals and the Anglo-Catholics — may have at times seemed venomous to the point of being unchristian. But each party was able to fight on the presumed ground that it was the genuine Church of England, while the other was aberrant. Each party thus found itself justifying a wide range of theological positions by essentially an identical practical stance: namely, that the true Church of England was parochial (and each party used its parishes as a base for defence against and attack upon the other), and that the parochial work of the church, including that of the occasional offices, had to be done effectively and conscientiously as evidence for the claim to historical and theological truth that each group was making for itself.[9] There resulted a healthy competition among the clergy to be good, indeed the best, parish priests. In consequence, apart from the occasional extreme instance, local churches ministered to their parishioners in much the same way. Slight differences — stoles or scarves, candles or flowers, altars or tables — did not matter greatly to the people, however much they were felt by church members, especially the clergy, to be vital.

At present, however, the Church of England seems to be losing contact with this profound sense of a parochial task. Formally it seems not to be struggling to discover what this might be in the light of social changes, although a large number of devoted parochial clergy are still trying, usually against the odds of pressure from the wider church. In place, therefore, of theological dispute based upon an agreed approach to pastoral ministry, the parties now seem to collude around mere theological argument. Care has in consequence to be taken when the word 'theological' is brandished in considerations of the pastoral practice of the occasional offices. For it seems to lack the content assigned to it by the common assumptions about such ministry which once prevailed.

Theological argument, necessary though it is, also needs

examining for the way in which it is being used. It can be
employed to avoid the work of ministry rather than to lead to
it. The view taken in this book is that the church, whether it
likes it or not, is still enmeshed in a series of significant ways
in the lives of ordinary men and women. Any theological
discussion, therefore, must include data that derive from the
practice of ministry with such people. When theology is used
as a means to avoid work, it is usually characterized by
mention of 'principles' or 'fundamentals'. One of the principles
or fundamentals, however, is that in the West the Christian
church has deliberately offered itself for handling people's
deepest, often irrational, emotions. Theological consequences
follow from that decision, which cannot be revoked by
serendipitous discovery of a so-called alternative (to some,
more pristine) set of principles. The interaction of the church
with its environment creates theological reflection. Perhaps
too much of this interaction is today seen in terms of the
individual. The church then becomes merely another facet of
the individual believer's life, with which he or she alone has
to interact. Such narcissism can scarcely have a future, since
it is an inevitably sterile encounter with a presumed self. But
one ministerial outcome is both pastoral and theological.
Since individuals and their link with the church are the focal
point of interpretation, the attempt is made to impose a
theological framework of understanding upon people so that
they can be believed by the church to be capable of receiving
ministry. But in so doing theological presumptions are only
confirmed and not explored. Pastoral concern for people as
human beings is reduced to manipulation, rather than to a
discernment of their intrinsic value to God and their
significance for the church.

Theological Indications for Ministry through the Occasional Offices

The church's self-understanding and its theological interpretation of God's world will be furthered in so far as the content
of Christian theology is scrutinized through the practice of
Christian ministry. The sacraments, for example, have been
seen to be both signs to the world and reflexive symbols to

the church. Theological learning will function in a similar way, in so far as it is informed by ideas that derive from the church's interactions with God's creation, and specifically with men and women in their everyday experience. Three useful, but often neglected or overlooked, aspects of such thinking are those of wisdom, representation and inclusive exclusiveness.

Donald Capps has developed a theory of 'Pastoral Care as Therapeutic Wisdom' in which he brings together the Wisdom tradition and Erikson's life-cycle theory. He describes the three major disorienting experiences of life as moral confusion, inability to grasp meaning, and severe suffering. These he sees as addressed respectively in three books of Wisdom— Proverbs, Ecclesiastes and Job.[10] From time to time the Wisdom tradition is explored in the church, but it seems to have little overt impact on contemporary ministry. While the world looks for wise men, Christian ministers seem more enthused by the aggressive image of the prophet or the self-ridiculing image of the clown. Neither of these stances is discredited. Prophetic discernment is a facet of any ministry, and wise folly is one view of pastoral care.[11] But the Wisdom tradition, perhaps in not so schematized a way as in Capps' approach, has some profound aspects, which constitute valuable referents for thinking about pastoral ministry. The realities of life, its opportunities, injustices, hopes and fears, are its chief topic. This tradition is located precisely where people feel themselves to be. Occasionally it declines into cynicism—an experience which is not unknown to ministers— but its basic orientation is to hope. It values everything, including the small and apparently insignificant things of everyday life. Theological interpretation, therefore, is based upon the simple stance of first trusting people and then offering them ideas about meaning. Using internal criteria from existing life and life-styles, this tradition checks them against a faith in God. It is thus always a theological attitude which enlarges the options in what is the case, rather than limiting them through presuppositions or diminishing the impact of available evidence. To magnify God it is not necessary to devalue human life.[12] Wisdom, therefore, is essentially a loving approach to God's world, since in so trusting mankind, God is classically presented as letting-be, which is the heart of the nature of divine love.[13]

The second model may be derived from Second Isaiah. This is a theological understanding of the idea of representation. In that text the notion of God's servant is amplified in a series of somewhat mysterious songs. The chief characteristic of this servant, however, is that he can accept delegation from God to be what God wishes him to be on his behalf.[14] To do this he does not initially have to be personally in touch with God. His vocation depends not upon his worthiness, spirituality or acceptability, but solely upon his being chosen by God as his representative. Hence, by a profound insight, the writer can claim that the enemy of God's people is God's anointed. Cyrus becomes the anointed prince, chosen by God to be his pastor (Isa. 24.28ff). In order to make such a claim, the prophet has to sustain certain other views: God is the only God, and people's behaviour, however inexplicable, cannot be ascribed to devotion to another; God is the creator of all things, and therefore is not preoccupied with his chosen people; this God is continually creating something new, in this instance a new exodus; and the suffering of God's people is, as it always has been, a vocation for the benefit of all mankind. Such themes seem vital as points of reference for any pastoral minister who can perceive that the church's focus of concern can never be those who are members of its congregations.

Thirdly, there is the question of the comprehensiveness of any theology. There is a natural tendency among religious people, from which Christians are not free, to affirm positions in order to exclude consideration of their converse and to make excited affirmations in order to eschew what is being denied. The history of Christian theism, for example, may be seen in this perspective.[15] One particularly acute form of this for the Christian is the struggle between each person's individuality and their corporate context. In the New Testament this striving comes primarily to the fore as the writer of the Fourth Gospel consistently affirms the individual and his decisions by giving them without fail a corporate context and significance.[16] So, for example, the individual is saved only in the context of the world's salvation as a whole

(John 3.16); the crucifixion of the one man is also his glorification in order to draw the whole world to him (John 12.37). Christian belief is marked by a powerful exclusiveness. The believer is called out from the rest of the world. But once acknowledged, this exclusive behaviour becomes utterly, and sometimes embarrassingly, inclusive. He is asked to recognize a form of representation for the very people from whom he has, by his act of faith, dissociated himself. This stance is one that the pastor has to pursue theologically for himself. For he faces it regularly in his daily encounters with individuals and the wider significance that each carries. He also requires some such approach to questions of his own personal individuality and how that is to be valued, not only for his day-to-day dealings with parishioners but, even more importantly, for all aspects of his ministry, when this is viewed *sub specie aeternitatis.*

These three models, which have been sketchily outlined, may help the pastor orient himself towards continuing ministry in the face of those pressures which were discussed earlier. They also provide points of contact between the minister's own spiritual life of prayer and its development and his public life as a live symbol. The near cynicism of the Wisdom writers will never be far from his experience. Nor will he be unfamiliar with the extraordinary vehicles that God can use to convey a message to the community of the faithful. And, as has been consistently argued, the way in which exclusive aspects of human life and of Christian witness may become implicitly inclusive, is something with which the minister, like the writer of the Fourth Gospel, permanently struggles. In this maelstrom of experience and reflection the minister may then notice that at various times Jesus Christ is understood as the wisdom of God, the servant of God, and finally as the crucified one who draws all to himself.

The five pressures, however, especially when they coincide, can prove overwhelming. Understanding may help, but two further parts of ministerial preparation are required: vision and learning. The emphasis in this book has been on seeing these brief encounters as processes through which people and minister go together. It is an interpretative—essentially

priestly—ministry.[17] The vision needed for such a ministry
may be of the opportunities presented in the most unlikely
guises. But equally requisite is a vision which encompasses
the process itself. Peter Selby has described the majesty and
the disaster that are integral to it. The pastoral relationship
introduces pastors, if only they can grasp this vision, to the
'public ills of the world as well as to the great themes of the
Christian faith'.[18] To hold such a vision in touch with reality
requires a commitment to the way of Christ and a firm grasp
on the fact of the church, as it exists by interaction between
itself and God's world.[19] Risking exploration through these
pastoral ministrations will enlarge the vision of the occasional
offices as well as that of the ministry of the Christian church.

As for training, this has been mentioned from time to time
in the course of the discussion. It has no magic of its own,
and operates under constraints. Practising clergy have only
limited time at their disposal for study in any field. And the
minister needs to sustain a wider perspective upon himself
and his work than is implied by specific learning about the
occasional offices. He has been described in this book
primarily as someone who is aware of his role and willing to
risk scrutiny and exploration of himself as a means to serving
the church's task. Mere acquisition of believed skills will not
greatly assist him. Such limitations are typically those which
indicate that a vocational model of learning is required rather
than an academic, or university style, approach.[20] The
academic approach (and the word is not used pejoratively) is
that of the university. There in theory all aspects of, and work
on, a topic are opened up and the student is required to draw
his own conclusions and argue for them. A vocational model,
by contrast, is tied to students with a specific role, for which
they need a consistent framework. Once this is discerned,
training—or better, development—is coherently linked
through the framework, and a range of approaches is
evaluated in the light of it. A reliable and adequate grasp of
the subject matter may be possible for students, without the
requirement that they step out of their professional role.[21]
Such training does not lead to the disowning of one's
responsibilities, but to a clearer, personal grasp of what they
might be and, what is more, what they might signify.

Vision and training, which themselves are not dissociated, may be directed to a common end—the better understanding and performance of Christian ministry and a recovery of the clergy's pastoral function in the light of the new demands that are made upon it by the contemporary world. To that end the occasional offices, fraught as they are with various practical and theological problems, may nevertheless be regarded as a means and not an unfortunate hindrance.

Notes

1. J. S. Stewart, *Heralds of God* (London, Hodder & Stoughton, 1946), p. 170: 'Beware the professional busy-ness which is but slackness in disguise.'
2. Monica Furlong in *New Christian,* 16th June 1966, p. 12.
3. E. J. Miller, 'Open systems revisited: a proposition about development and change', in W. G. Lawrence, ed., *Exploring Individual and Organisational Boundaries* (London, Wiley, 1979), pp. 217ff. Citation from p. 218.
4. *TPT,* pp. 19ff.
5. Contrast the understanding of professionalism in A. Russell, *The Clerical Profession* (London, SPCK, 1980), with that proposed in *The Continuing Education of the Church's Ministers,* GS Misc 122 (London, CIO, 1978).
6. Habgood, *Church and Nation,* pp. 93ff.
7. S. Ranson, A. Bryman and B. Hinings, *Clergy, Ministers and Priests* (London, RKP, 1977).
8. D. Jenkins, *The British: Their Identity and Their Religion* (London, SCM, 1975), pp. 59ff.
9. See, e.g., G. R. Balleine, *A History of the Evangelical Party in the Church of England* (London, Church Bookroom Press, 1951). K. Leech and R. Williams, ed., *Essays Catholic and Anglican* (London, Bowedean Press, 1983), especially R. Arguile, 'Parishes and people', pp. 131ff, and V. Pitt, 'The Oxford Movement: a case of cultural distortion', pp. 205ff. An overview of the basic theological issue may be found in S. W. Sykes, *The Integrity of Anglicanism* (Oxford, Mowbray, 1978).
10. D. Capps, *Life-Cycle Theory and Pastoral Care* (Philadelphia, Fortress, 1983), pp. 99f.
11. For 'prophet' see *TPT,* pp. 52ff. On 'wise folly' see A. V. Campbell, *Rediscovering Pastoral Care* (London, DLT, 1981).
12. J. L. Crenshaw, *Old Testament Wisdom* (London, SCM, 1982).

13. W. H. Vanstone, *Love's Endeavour, Love's Expense* (London, DLT, 1977).
14. *TPT*, pp. 53ff.
15. J. Macquarrie, *In Search of Deity* (London, SCM, 1984).
16. C. F. D. Moule, 'The Individualism of the Fourth Gospel', *Novum Testamentum* 5 (1962), pp. 171ff.
17. *TPT*, pp. 13ff.
18. Selby, *Liberating God*, p. 8.
19. Carr, 'A teaching church'.
20. I owe this distinction to discussion with the late Dr P. M. Turquet. Some of the thinking here was developed with the late R. W. Herrick for the Bishop of Chelmsford.
21. *TPT*, pp. 87ff. For a model see the so-called 'Balint groups': R. Gosling, D. Miller, P. M. Turquet and D. L. Woodhouse, *The Use of Small Groups in Training* (Hertford, Codicote Press, 1967).

Index

Age Concern 122
Ainsworth-Smith, I. 124
Allen, R. 63, 84
Arguile, R. 139

Backer, B. A. 124
Badham, L. 124
Badham, P. 124
Baker, T. G. A. 112, 124
Balleine, G. R. 139
baptism 37ff, 63ff
Barker, D. L. 18, 102
Beattie, J. 18
Bede 23, 32
Bell, D. 17f
Berkouwer, G. 58
Bicknell, E. J. 58
Bion, W. R. 102
Bliss, K. 18
Bocock, R. J. 57
Bonhoeffer, D. 45
Boroborio, D. 57
Bowlby, J. 32
Browning, R. 5
Bryman, A. 139

Campbell, A. V. 139
Capps, D. 135, 139
Carkhuff, R. R. 18
Carr, A. W. xiii, 44, 140
Chelmsford, Diocese of 53ff
Chitty, D. J. 45
Colman, A. D. and L. L. 102
confirmation 24f

Corbin, M. 18
counselling 12ff
covenant 75f
creation 52f
Crenshaw, J. L. 139
Crichton, J. D. 84
cross 53
Cruse 124
Cuming, G. J. 97, 103

Davis, M. 32
death 104ff
dependency 20ff
Dominian, J. 93, 100, 102f
Donne, J. 124
Douglas, M. 44

Erikson, E. H. 22, 32
Eucharist 39

Fairbairn, W. R. D. 45
family, church as 79, 85
fantasy 102
Feifel, H. 123
Fisher, J. D. C. 57
Fox, M. J. xii
Frankham, H. F. xii
funerals 104ff
Furlong, M. 139

Gennep, A. van 18, 26
Gill, R. 57
Gluckmann, M. 18
Gorer, G. 44, 102, 123

Gosling, R. 140
Grainger, R. 57
Green, M. 102f
Guggenbuhl-Craig, A. 18

Habgood, J. 17, 139
Hannon, N. 124
Hare-Duke, M. 45
Hay, D. 17
Hebblethwaite, P. 3, 5
Hebert, A. G. 57
Hennessy, P. J. 124
Henson, H. H. 63, 84
Herrick, R. W. 140
Hewitt, G. H. G. 84
Hick, J. H. 124
Hines, B. 139
Hocking, M. 102

identity of church 35f
Isaiah 42, 136

Jagger, P. J. 84
James, E. 67f, 84
Jenkins, D. 139
Jenson, R. W. 44
John Paul II 102
Jones, C. 57
Jung, C. G. 32

Kavanagh, A. 5, 57
Kee, A. 45
Kelly, J. N. D. 57
Klein, M. 45
Koets, P. J. 84
Kübler-Ross, E. 31, 123
Küng, H. 44

Lampe, G. W. H. 64
Laplanche, J. 44
Lash, N. 45
Lawrence, W.G. 31, 139
Leach, E. R. 18
Leech, K. 139

Lewis, C. A. 85
Loewenich, W. van 58
Long, C. H. 84
Lowther Clarke, W. G. 102
Luther, M. 22, 57f

McCarthy, J. B. 124
Macquarrie, J. 140
Maldonado, L. 5
Margolis, O. S. 124
marriage 86ff
Marriage Guidance Council 97
Marshall, P. J. xii
Martin, D. 5, 17
Martos, J. 57
Marwick, A. 32
Maurice, F. D. 40, 45, 75, 84
Middleton, R. 18
Miller, D. 140
Miller, E. J. 31f, 84, 139
ministry 11f, 127ff
mission 10f
Mitford, J. 123
Moltmann, J. 44f, 124
Morris, C. 102
Moss, B. 84f
Moule, C. F. D. 140
Musgrove, F. 18

Needham, G. xi
North, M. 18, 45, 57

pair, power of the 87f
Parkes, C. M. 31
pastoral, meaning of 2ff
Paton, D. 84
Perham, M. 82, 84, 98, 103
Pickering, W. S. F. 17
Pitt, V. 139
Platten, S. 102
Pocknee, C. E. 84
Pontalis, J-B. 44
Power, D. 5, 57
projection 35f, 38f

Quick, O. C. 40, 45, 76, 84

Rahner, K. 45
Ranson, S. 139
Reed, B. D. 17f, 31, 84, 116,
  124
religion 9ff, 52ff
resurrection 53
Rice, A. K. 32, 84
rites 14f, 19ff
ritual 16
Roman Catholic Marriage
  Advisory Commission 97
Ross, S. A. 124
Runcie, R. A. K. 102
Russell, A. 139
Russell, N. A. 124

sacraments 46ff
Schillebeeckx, E. 44
Schneider, L. 17
Selby, P. 18, 140
Shakespeare, W. 22
Shapiro, E. R. 103
Speck, P. W. 124
Spiegel, Y. 31
Stevens, R. 32
Stevens, T. J. xii
Stewart, J. S. 139
Sykes, S. W. 35f, 44, 139
systems 28ff

Taft, R. 57
Taylor, J. V. 45

thanksgiving, sense of 78f
Tillich, P. 58
time 15
Torrie, M. 124
Towler, R. 17
Toynbee, A. 123
transitional objects 25f
transitions 22ff
Truax, C. B. 18
Turner, V. 18
Turquet, P. M. 140

undertakers 108ff

Vanstone, W. H. 140
Virgo, L. 18

Waal, E. de 85
Wagner, G. 44
Wainwright, G. 57
Wallbridge, D. 32
weddings 90ff
Williams, R. 139
Winnicott, D. W. 25f, 32, 45,
  103
wisdom 135f
Woodhouse, D. L. 140
worship, management of 116ff
Wright, D. 45
Wright, F. 77, 84

Yarnold, E. J. 57

Also by Wesley Carr

THE PRIESTLIKE TASK
A Model for Developing and Training
the Church's Ministry

'The value of this book is that it invites us to take
the Church of England seriously, to ask what is its
task in England today, to form a strategy of
ministry to fulfil that task, and to be clear about
what we are doing in parishes, deaneries, dioceses
and so on. It certainly has made me think and
given me new perspectives of thought.'
Peter Toon, Church of England Newspaper

'Provokes thought . . . it pioneers in relating insights
derived from the social sciences to ecclesiastical
questions. Its author is undeniably a man of great
intelligence and integrity with a passion to help
the Church to be more effective.'
David L. Edwards, Church Times

Also available in this series

LETTING GO
Caring for the Dying and Bereaved

Ian Ainsworth-Smith and Peter Speck

'This book is quite admirable. It really says
everything to enable the pastor to minister
effectively to the dying and the bereaved. It
should be studied closely by all ministers, lay
and ordained.' *Hospital Chaplain*

'What gives the book its especial value is the wide
experience of two hospital chaplains which lies
behind it, and their ability to put this alongside the
findings of people like Pincus, Parkes and
Lindemann, together with their frequent reference to
case studies which greatly illuminate the text, and
to rites and customs in different societies from
our own, and in other religions than
Christianity.' *Theology*

'Various issues, especially concerning
communication, are discussed with a sensitivity that
might be as helpful to medical and nursing students
as to ministers.' *British Medical Journal*

'A splendidly concise and practical distillation of
much recent thinking and pastoral
practice.' *Church Times*

Also available in this series

MAKE OR BREAK

An Introduction to Marriage Counselling

Jack Dominian

'This is not a book to be read and put aside. It can
be a valuable tool in the busy pastor's workshop
and can be consulted confidently and
frequently. Dr Dominian's underlying
principles are solid and his guidance wise
and sensitive.' *Churchman*

'A very useful first reader for anybody likely to be
approached with marriage problems. To the
marriage guidance counsellor in training I
recommend it for general background
information. Many of the basic principles of
counselling are set out clearly, and useful
material will be found in the chapters on social and
psychological factors, phases in marriage, and on
particular recurring problems such as alcoholism,
depression and violence.' *Marriage Guidance*

'Eminently readable . . . a simple introduction to the
process and understanding of counselling for any
professional working with people who seek help in
the distress that results from disturbances in their
emotional relationships.' *British Medical Journal*